Domestic Life in Virginia

❦

In the Seventeenth Century

Annie Lash Jester

CLEARFIELD COMPANY

Originally Published 1957

Reprinted for
Clearfield Company, Inc. by
Genealogical Publishing Company Inc.
Baltimore, Maryland
1994

International Standard Book Number 0-8063-4512-8

*Jamestown 350th Anniversary Historical Booklet
Number 17*

PART I

LAYING THE HEARTHSTONES

INTRODUCTION

Successful colonization, contingent upon a stable domestic life, was quickened in Virginia with the coming of the gentlewoman Mrs. Lucy Forest and her maid Ann Burras, who with Mrs. Forest's husband Thomas, arrived in the second supply, 1608, following the planting of the colony at Jamestown, 13 May 1607.

The possibility of finding a source of wealth in the new world, such as the Spanish had found in Mexico and Peru, and the more urgent need of finding a route to the East and securing this through the development of colonies across the seas, had motivated the several expeditions, begun with the unsuccessful settlement at Roanoke Island in 1585. Coupled with these reasons, for colonizing in the new world, was an ever expanding population in England, and the ancient law of entail, which limited possession of large landed estates to the eldest sons; younger sons and the scions of the middle classes were left with exceedingly limited opportunities or means of attaining estates in England, or, for that matter, of ever bettering their condition. Also, if England was to sustain its existing population, the nation must have sources of raw materials other than the dwindling supplies in the land, and it must have also outlets for the wares of the artisans.

Thus, while the hope of wealth in one form or another was a factor in the settlement of Virginia, a prerequisite to attainment, also taken into account by the promoters of expeditions, was the establishment of homes in a new land. Homes would serve as stabilizers for permanent bases, from which could be carried on the trade essential to England's rising position as a leading power.

Notwithstanding hardship, discouragement and sickness, the firm resolution of the English succeeded. Their determination,

1

as shown in their several attempts at colonization, culminated eventually in a colonial homeland, which offered to gentlemen adventurers the lure of the unknown, as well as the prospect of land, and, to the many unemployed craftsmen a demand for their labor and privileges which could not be had by the average man in England.

Withal, the fireside became the bulwark for the great new venture. And, fortunate it was that such a base had been established, for, by the middle of the seventeenth century, many scions of the English upper classes were forced into exile because of the Civil wars, which reached their climax in the beheading of Charles I. A number of the King's loyal subjects found havens in Virginia and not only managed to bring with them some of the family wealth, but also their important connections with the trading enterprises, which gave another impetus to the colonial undertaking.

The silent part of women, ever in the background in the colony, but overseeing orderly households, comforting the men in discouragement and, at the same time carrying on the perpetual cycle of child bearing, was an immeasurable contribution. They braved the unknown to be at the sides of their mates and, as the prospering colony during the passing years of the century increased their responsibilities and burdens, they readily assumed the new tasks. Not least among these was that of household executive: managing servants, seeing that they as well as the family were clothed, fed and attended in their sicknesses, supervising spinning, weaving, garment making and generally maintaining a hub for the operation of plantations ranging from 100 acres to those of several thousands.

To the Englishman, the basis for wealth and position was a large landed estate. News from Virginia had spread the information that great fertile lands, sparsely inhabited by the natives, were available. Thus, valid expectations sent the women thither, some with their husbands, some to join their husbands, some to

2

follow their sweethearts and, by 1620, some to find husbands among the men who were toiling to establish the Colony firmly and longing for the comforts of their own firesides.

The first wedding in Virginia took place in 1608, not long after the arrival of Mrs. Forest and her maid, who, as may be surmised, did not long remain a maid. John Laydon, who had come as a laborer in 1607, took her, a girl fourteen years old, then of marriageable age, for a bride. In 1625, they were living with their four daughters in Elizabeth City Corporation.

THE FIRST HOMES

The Laydon marriage probably had taken place in the rough little church built at Jamestown within the stockade, which enclosed also the first houses of the settlers along with a guard-house and a storehouse. The stockade, actually a triangular fort built as protection against the natives, was erected of a succession of upright logs, some twelve feet in height and sharpened to a point. The small buildings within, patterned after the simple homes of the peasantry in England, were built of available material. Beams were cut from the trees in the forests close by, the timbers being held together with pegs. The uprights were interwoven with osiers or stout vines and, on these wattles, was daubed the clay and mud found in the surrounding area, which the colonists had mixed with reeds from the marshes. Coatings of this applied both outside and inside, when dry, made thick, though perhaps fragile walls. Nevertheless, they shut out temporarily, at least, the chill winds and the summer heat. Material for chimneys was not then available, and the colonists made do the ample openings in the roofs thatched with reeds. Sometimes, skins were attached on the outer sides of these openings and flapped over the hole, in a heavy storm, to shut out the rain. Openings for light were closed with sliding panels. Shallow wells within the stockade supplied water, not always unpolluted.

The tinder-like material, with which these first buildings were

3

constructed, together with the open central fires, made them a prey to flames in January, 1608, which shortly were out of control. The reeds, with which the roofs were thatched, merely fed the blaze which spread so rapidly that even the palisades were destroyed. The colonists lost practically everything, including arms, clothing, bedding and provisions held by individuals. Reverend Robert Hunt suffered the loss of his collection of books.

By 1609, a number of women passengers were included among those who departed from England on nine ships, comprising the largest expedition ever sent to Virginia. Reverend Richard Buck brought with him his wife, and although they were among those marooned for nine months on the Bermuda Islands following the wreck there of the *Seaventure*, both survived the hardships encountered, and established a home at Jamestown and reared a family. Temperance Flowerdieu, aged about fourteen years, arrived in 1609 on the *Falcon*, but presumably returned to England, shortly to come back, in 1618, as the wife of Sir George Yeardley. Thomas Dunthorne's wife came in the *Triall*, 1610, and their servant Elizabeth Joones was among those on the *Seaventure* who eventually reached Virginia in the *Patience*, 1610. Sisley Jordan, later wife of William Farrar, came in the *Swan*, 1610.

By the time the second contingent of women had arrived, America's first industry, glass making, had been established and the colonists had built some twenty houses, providing also for themselves a well of "excellent sweet water" within the fort. The conditions of living were somewhat improved. The fragile walls of the church, having begun to crumble, were renewed and a block house was built on the neck of the Island, to which point the savages were permitted to come for trade, but were prohibited from further passage by a garrison kept there. When not otherwise employed, the men spent their time fashioning clapboard and wainscoting from the trees cut from the surrounding forests.

4

Finding their limited food supplies spoiled by mold or eaten by a horde of rats, the offspring of rodents which arrived also on the first ships, the colonists were forced to the necessity of "living off the country." In the spring they planted some thirty or forty acres hoping for a plentiful crop before midsummer. Also, upon taking an inventory of livestock, they found in all sixty odd pigs, the offspring of three sows which they originally possessed; and some 500 chickens roamed around their habitations, feeding from the countryside. Yet, in order not to tax this supply, sixty or eighty of the colonists were sent down the river to live on oysters and other seafood, obtainable at and near Old Point. Sturgeon was plentiful; in fact, there being a greater supply than could be used, some of the surplus was dried, then pounded, mixed with the roe and sorrel to provide both bread and meat. Also, an edible root called *tockwough* (tuckahoe, a tuberous plant growing in fresh marshes, with a root similar to that of a potato) was gathered, and after the Indian fashion, pounded into a meal from which bread was made.

In order to conserve their scarce food supply, the colonists sought to acquaint themselves with the use of the native resources. To this end, a number of the settlers were billetted with the Indians. They not only learned to distinguish the edible roots, berries, leafy plants and fruits, and how to prepare them, but found the whereabouts of Indian trails, the location of their villages, and fields where they cultivated corn, beans, and *apooke* (tobacco).

SICKNESS AND DISCOURAGEMENT

Yet, a scarce two years in the wilderness hardly equipped the Englishmen to cope with the altogether new situations which they encountered. Aside from the lack of adequate provisions for the heavy diet in beef, mutton and pork to which they were accustomed in England, there were at least two months of hot,

5

humid weather to which they were not acclimated. Moreover, during this period, the "sickness"—probably malaria and yellow fever from the West Indies and diarrhea from polluted drinking-water—was rampant. Also the hostility of certain of the Indians increased the death toll. Debilitated, discouraged and fearful of the savages, the survivors hovered together at Jamestown. By May 1610, all of their livestock had been consumed, including hogs, hens, goats, sheep and even a horse. Finally, the sixty living began to trade their weapons to the savages in exchange for food.

This was the state of the colony when 150 adventurers—men, women and children—marooned for nine months on the Bermuda Islands after the wreck of the *Seaventure,* arrived in the *Patience* and the *Deliverance* commanded by Sir Thomas Gates and Sir George Somers. The newcomers, who already had passed through a harrowing experience, faced a forlorn situation in the land of their destination; and so their leaders concurred in a decision to return to England. But, Lord De La Warr's timely arrival, with three ships exceedingly well furnished with all necessaries, changed the outlook. Here were not only the means of survival but resources for some stable home life. Several of the women who had sailed in the 1609 expedition reached Jamestown ahead of their shipwrecked husbands, who had accompanied the official party on the *Seaventure.* Among these were Mrs. Joane Peirce, wife of Captain William Peirce, and their daughter Joane, who arrived at Jamestown, 1609, on the *Blessing.*

RELIEF

One of Lord De La Warr's first commands ordered the building of a number of houses, since he found the fragile buildings erected of unseasoned timbers, after the fire, already in a state of decay. The roofs of these new dwellings were covered with boards and the sides were fortified against the weather with Indian mats.

The following May, 1611, Sir Thomas Dale reached Jamestown with three ships, men, cattle and provisions for a year. Four months later, six ships under Sir Thomas Gates, who had carried back to England news of the desperate straits of the colony in 1610, arrived with a complement of 300 men, 100 kine and other livestock, with munitions and all manner of provisions.

Dale, a hard taskmaster, in his capacity as Marshal, put the settlers under a military regime and, in requiring a schedule of work for everyone, succeeded in establishing the colony on a firm basis. He ordered at once the repair of the Church, the storehouse and other buildings, adding a munitions house, a building in which to cure sturgeon, a cattle-barn and a stable.

In order to broaden the base of the colony, Dale at once set about seeking a suitable location for a new town, which he located on the neck of land since changed into an island by the Dutch Gap canal, and later known as Farrar's Island. At the site of the projected town, laid out on a seven acre enclosed plat, and called Henrico, he raised watchtowers at four corners, built a wooden church and several storehouses, laid off streets on which frame dwellings were erected, with the first stories, probably the foundations, built of brick. This is the earliest mention of the use of bricks for home building in Virginia. Also, five houses were erected on the banks of the James River, the dwellers agreeing to act as sentinels for approach to the town by water.

The elements, however, favored the new town no more than Jamestown, and the buildings were constantly in need of repair. A hospital was projected for location at the new town and its building begun. At the site, also, a college for the education of the Indians was planned, and iron works were erected at Falling Creek, a portion of the profits from which, under agreement, was to defray the cost of operation of the proposed college. As is well known, the Indians, in an attempt to wipe out the colony in 1622, practically obliterated the town.

Terms agreed upon, in the Virginia Company at the beginning of the settlement, stipulated that there should be no individual assignments of land during the first seven years. The communal plan, under which the colonists lived through these years, was terminated while Dale ruled the colony; a policy was adopted of assigning rights for a hundred acres to every individual who had come to Virginia, before 1616, with the intention of planting (settling). This acreage could be doubled under certain conditions. Those who came, after 1616, were entitled to fifty acres each, provided they paid their own passages. Similarly, each could claim an additional fifty acres in the name of every person whose passage he paid. This was known as the headright system of granting land. Thus, a man with a wife, three children and two servants, was entitled to 350 acres. Not only did these generous provisions, for the acquisition of landed estates, lure settlers to the new world, but they provided a sound base for the beginning of a secure domestic life in the colony.

Unfortunately, there is no complete list of the women who came to Virginia prior to 1616, but, in addition to those heretofore named, the presence of others is recorded. Joane Salford, wife of Robert Salford of Elizabeth City, came by 1611, and Salford's sister Sarah reached Virginia at the same time, or just a year or so later. Susan, wife of John Collins of West and Shirley Hundred, came in the *Treasurer*, 1613. Elizabeth, wife of Lieutenant Albiano Lupo, came in the *George,* 1616, and little Susan Old was brought by her cousin Richard Biggs, when she was only two years of age; eight years later she was reported living with the Biggs family in Charles City Corporation. Martha Key was with her husband Thomas by 1616. Rachel Davis joined her husband Captain James Davis before 1616, and their son Thomas later settled in Isle of Wight and Upper Norfolk (Nansemond) Counties, taking out land patents, in the name of his parents as old planters. Mary Flint, wife of Captain Thomas

8

Flint of the area which later became Warwick County, was the widow of Robert Beheathland, who had come to Virginia with the first settlers in 1607. Beheathland's wife arrived some time before 1616 and they had two daughters, Mary and Dorothy, who married and left Virginia descendants. Izabella,—three times married, first to Richard Pace, second, to William Perry and third to George Menefie came to the colony before 1616.

The Company's Tenants, Their Supplies and Their Wives

After the first settlement at Jamestown, the Virginia Company recognized that youthful, hearty young men were essential in the new land, in order to cope with the wilderness. Inducements were offered, both in passage across the seas at Company expense, and in supplies and equipment furnished each man. Moreover, by 1616, there was the lure of land at the end of the required seven-year tenure of service and the hope of becoming a planter. Probably, articles of indenture were drawn for these tenants as they were later between colonists and their servants.

The cost of sending and supplying these young men was a considerable sum. Passage alone cost £6 and, together with supplies furnished and freight on them, the total cost of bringing a youth to Virginia amounted to £20. Even if an adventurer paid his own passage he was advised to come with the same "necessaries." In apparel, each needed a Monmouth cap, three falling bands (large loose collars), three shirts, a waistcoat, a suit of canvas (work clothes), a suit of frieze and a suit of cloth, also three pairs of Irish stockings, four pairs of shoes, a pair of garters, a dozen points, a pair of canvas sheets, canvas to make a bed and a bolster, to be filled in Virginia and serving for two men, canvas to make a bed enroute, also for two men, a coarse rug (covering) at sea for two men.

In food the adventurer needed eight bushels of meal, two bushels of peas, eight bushels of oatmeal, a gallon of wine, a gallon of oil and two gallons of vinegar. In armor, he was advised

9

to possess a complete light suit, a musket, a sword, a belt and a bandoleer, twenty pounds of powder and sixty pounds of shot or lead, together with a pistol and goose-shot.

For a group of six men the following tools were deemed essential: five broad-hoes, five narrow-hoes, two broadaxes, five felling-axes, four handsaws, a whipsaw with equipment for filing, two hammers, three shovels, two spades, two augers, six chisels, two piercing tools, three gimlets, two hatchets, two frowes, two handbills, a grindstone, nails of all sorts and two pickaxes.

Household utensils to be used by six persons included an iron pot, a kettle, a large frying-pan, a gridiron, two skillets, a spit, platters, dishes and spoons of wood.

There was a charge for sugar, spice and fruit to be supplied on the voyage. Moreover, if the company was made up of a number of persons, they were advised to bring, in addition to the above: nets, hooks and lines for fishing, cheese, kine and goats.

By 1618, the Virginia Company had set aside 3000 acres of land in each of the four corporations, Elizabeth City, James City, Henrico and Charles City, where they settled these young men known as the Company's tenants. Half of the profit from their labors went to the Company to defray costs of Colonial government. However, Governor Sir George Yeardley realized that far too few of these substantial workers, inured to the climate and the wilderness, were satisfied to remain in the Colony. He, forthwith, reported the situation to Sir Edwin Sandys, then Treasurer of the Company, who then proposed that one hundred "maids young and uncorrupt" be sent to the Colony to become wives, stipulating that their passage would be paid by the Company if they married the Company's tenants; otherwise, their passage money should be reimbursed to the Company by the planter-husbands whom they had chosen.

By 17 May, 1620, ninety young women had come to the Colony under these arrangements, having embarked in the *London Merchant* and the *Jonathan*. The following year, an additional

fifty-seven young women came in three ships, the *Marmaduke,*
the *Warwick* and the *Tiger.* The Virginia Company reported to
Governor Yeardley that "extraordinary diligence" and care had
been exercised in the choice of the maids, and that none had
been received, who had other than excellent reputations in their
communities. They further reported that they had provided
"young, handsome and honestly educated maids."

Evidently, there was no problem in arranging marriages, and
report went back to England that among the last fifty-seven sent
to Virginia, many had been married, before the ships, on which
they arrived, had departed from the Colony for the return voyage.
But, whom they and the others married is not known, nor are the
fates of the 147 young women who came to fill gaps in home
life, known. Some were certainly slain in the massacre, others
must have died of the sickness soon after coming, for Governor
Berkeley later estimated that four out of five persons died, in the
early years, shortly after arrival, especially if they came in late
spring or summer when the sickness took its toll.

Supplies for a Particular Plantation

In an effort to reduce the financial burden of colonization resting solely upon the Virginia Company, and at the same time to
satisfy some of the shareholders, who were complaining of no
profit from their investment, their Council sitting in London,
inaugurated a policy of assigning thousands of acres for "particular plantations." These acreages were promised to shareholders
and other promoters, who agreed to transport colonists to Virginia and keep them supplied. Usually several promoters joined
in assuming the costs of such adventures and, thus, the Company
was altogether relieved of the cost and responsibility of settlement. In this category were the plantations at Martin's Hundred,
Berkeley, Smith's (Southampton) Hundred and Newport News.
Thomas Southey, who outfitted a ship and set out from England with his wife, six children and ten servants, came with great

11

expectations, having indicated his desire that the Company would assign to him a "particular plantation." His ship arrived safely in Virginia but before his hopes were realized, he and three of his children had died. However, one of his surviving daughters was the progenitor of a well known Eastern Shore family.

The settlement of Berkeley Hundred as a "particular plantation" was agreed upon, in 1619, with Captain John Woodliffe. The promoters, one of whom was John Smith of Nibley, England, soon became dissatisfied with Woodliffe's management of the project and revoked his commission, assigning a similar commission to William Tracy. In 1620, Tracy booked fifty colonists, twelve of whom were women, to come over in the *Supply*. The ship' was exceedingly well furnished with necessaries of every description that might be of use in his undertaking. Every item in the cargo on the ship of sixty tons burden is listed from onions to millstones. A resumé will give some idea of the wealth of commodities brought to Virginia in 1620. Among the implements useful for clearing land were pickaxes, felling-axes, squaring-axes, spades, weeding-hoes, scythes, reap-hooks. Grindstones and two French millstones were brought along with 22,500 nails, an anvil and two sieves for making gunpowder.

Material for making garments included linen of several grades, blue linen for facing doublets, dowlas, canvas for sheets and shirts. Ready for use were breeches of russet leather with leather linings, 100 Monmouth caps (round caps without a brim used by soldiers and sailors), 200 pairs of shoes of seven sizes, 100 pairs of knit socks, 100 pairs of Irish stockings, falling-bands, which were the large loose collars that fell about the neck replacing the stiff ruff of the sixteenth century. Accessories included glass beads, buttons, thread, both brown and black, twelve dozen yards of gartering, bone combs, scissors, shears and tailors' shears.

Among the utensils were trenchers (wooden plates or trays), bread-baskets, wooden spoons, porridge dishes, saucers and four dozen platters. For food there was wheat, butter, cheese, white peas, dried malt (probably for making beer), oatmeal, sugar, Irish beef, salted beef, pork and codfish, flitches of bacon, biscuit and a separate item of pap (mush) for indentured servants. Spices brought over included pepper, ginger, cinnamon, nutmeg, cloves, mace, and in the dried fruits there were dates, raisins, currants, prunes. A single variety in nuts is listed in a quantity of almonds, certainly a luxury in the colony in 1620.

For the household and various uses on the plantation there were barrels of tar and pitch, six hogsheads of baysalt (i.e. salt evaporated from sea water), 102 pounds of soap, ten gallons of oil, candles, wire candle-holders, lanterns and bellows. There were drugs and physic for the indisposed. Spring planting had not been overlooked for the ship brought a quantity of seeds in parsnips, carrots, cabbage, turnips, lettuce, onions, mustard and garlic.

For protection there were corslets, muskets, swords, lead and powder. Six bandoleers were listed; they were belts with loops holding pierced metal cases which held the matches for firing the powder which set off the charge in guns. The matches mentioned were actually slow burning fuses, as the modern match did not come into use until the nineteenth century.

Tragedy followed closely upon this auspicious second start for Berkeley Hundred. William Tracy was dead by 8 April 1621 and his wife Mary died the same year. Their daughter Joyce, who had married Captain Nathaniel Powell, was slain with her husband in the Indian massacre of 1622. A son Thomas who survived returned to England.

Of the twelve women named in the passenger list of the *Supply*, Joane Greene failed to make the trip and also, probably, Frances Page, whose husband was reported not to have come with the party, although he was booked. Frances Greville, a young gentlewoman, a cousin of the Tracys, was married by 1621 to young Nathaniel West, son of Lord De La Warr. Shortly becoming a widow, she thereafter married, as his second wife, the cape-mer-

13

chant Abraham Peirsey and upon his death, 1626, she became the wife of Captain Samuel Mathews of "Denbigh" on the Warwick River. William Finch, who brought over his wife and daughter Frances, was dead by 1622, and the widow shortly thereafter became the wife of Captain John Flood and the mother of three sons and a daughter. Jane Rowles, with her husband Richard, was slain and, though Joane Coopey and her son Anthony died, the daughter Elizabeth survived. Elizabeth Webb married in Virginia, and Isabel Gifford had been wed to Adam Raymer while the *Supply* was on the high seas.

The Magazine Ships

As has been previously indicated, all supplies, sent to the Colony during the first ten years, were paid for through the Company's treasury, but so great was the financial burden, particularly since the Colony was not yielding the profit anticipated, that a different arrangement was sought, in 1617. There was organized within the Company a "Society of Particular Adventurers for Traffic with the People of Virginia in Joint Stock." This was known as the Magazine, to which members of the Virginia Company contributed such sums as they were willing to venture. In practice, it was an association of private investors who, upon return of the ship that had been sent stocked to Virginia, divided the profits from the sale of goods and the tobacco returned on the ships, according to their investment in the enterprise.

The first of these ships to arrive in the Colony was the *Susan*, a vessel of small tonnage, with a cargo restricted to clothing of which the colonists ever stood in great need. Abraham Peirsey was in charge as Cape-Merchant and it was his responsibility also to dispose of the cargo at a price that would bring a profit to the promoters. The exchange, of course, was in tobacco or sassafras, the only two commodities at the time, which could be disposed of in England at a profit. Evidently, Peirsey was successful in his bargaining, for upon his return to England in the

14

Susan, he came back the following year with the second magazine ship, the *George,* which was delayed five months and in consequence unloaded a damaged cargo. Although during the remainder of the Company's tenure in Virginia, until June 1624, transportation of supplies, supposedly was restricted to the magazine ships, the vessels of private adventurers often reached the Colony with articles which were in the luxury class such as sweetmeats, sack (wine from southern Europe) and strong waters (liquor). The Dutch probably were the chief promoters of this trade, which England sought unsuccessfully to prohibit, as diverting the tobacco trade from the realm and diminishing the royal customs.

The Muster of the Inhabitants of Virginia, January, 1625

The dissolution of the Virginia Company in London, May 1624, left the colony without restriction to independent traders, who shortly began to respond to the colonists' eagerness for supplies from overseas. There is, however, a record of the Colony at the conclusion of the Company's administration taken just ahead of the influx of the accelerated trade.

As the Company was about to be dissolved, Captain John Harvey (later as Sir John Harvey, Governor of Virginia) was sent over to obtain exact information as to the number of people in Virginia, their names, where they lived and what supplies and arms they possessed. The document preserved in the British Public Record Office shows to what degree the planters had spread their homes along both banks of the James River from Henrico to Elizabeth City and Kecoughtan at the confluence of the James River with the Chesapeake Bay (this point now Hampton Roads) and on the Eastern Shore. In addition to the names of all persons living in the colony, the ages of many are given, together with the times of their arrival, and the names of the ships on which they came. Also, those recently deceased are listed.

The 1232 persons living in Virginia, January, 1625, dwelt at twenty-five locations. Several of these were large plantations, such as Peirsey's Hundred, Mr. Treasurer's (George Sandys'), Martin's Hundred, Captain Roger Smith's, Captain Samuel Mathews', Mr. Crowder's, Mr. Blaney's and Newport News, where colonists lived in groups, presumably as employees for the promotion of extensive enterprises. As previously mentioned a number of these colonists at Henrico, James City, Charles City and Elizabeth City were living on the Company's land. Yet, many at this time dwelt upon their own acreages, assigned to them individually in patents of record in a list sent to England the following year. For instance. Lieutenant John Chisman and his brother Edward were living at Kecoughtan on their patent of 200 acres, as was Pharoah Flinton who had been assigned an 150 acre plot, and John Bush with his 300 acres, where he dwelt with his wife, two children and two servants. For protection against the Indians, palisades had been erected at a number of the plantations.

Staples on hand are listed for every household, including corn, peas, beans, oatmeal, fish, the latter both smoked and in brine. Besides, many of the planters owned swine, poultry, goats and cattle. A few luxuries were mentioned such as a flitch of bacon, cheese and oil. For protection, the colonists possessed armor such as had been used in England, but which probably proved to be of little use against the stealthy natives in thickly wooded areas. Nevertheless, there were whole suits of armor, including headpieces, coats of mail and coats of plate and jack-coats (thickly padded jackets). The guns were of various types. Many apparently were of the older design and the charge had to be fired by the application of a fuse; others had been fixed with the more up-to-date firing mechanism attached to the gun. There were also matchlocks, snaphaunce pieces, pistols, swords and hangers (cutlasses). For the larger plantation there were small cannon, called murderers, usually placed at the bow of a ship to prevent boarding, falconets and petronels. The matches mentioned were the slow-burning fuses, kept by a soldier in his bandoleer. Once ignited, these "matches" kept a smouldering fire and could be used again and again. Pirates were accustomed to stick them lighted in their beards and hair, not to give a ferocious look, but for convenience.

Powder and lead also were on hand in many households, for life, on the edge of a wilderness with stealthy Indians frequently lurking about, was hazardous in the extreme. Men who worked in the fields took fowling pieces with them and, at times, armed guards were stationed to be on the lookout, and warn the workers in case of danger.

Among other possessions listed were the houses of the planters, their boats—barks, shallops and skiffs being named—and, at George Sandys' plantation across from Jamestown, a house for silkworms had been framed. The prolific growth of mulberry trees, about the Indian settlements and elsewhere, encouraged the English to conclude that Virginia was an ideal location for development of the silk industry. Greatly encouraged from England, the colonists made earnest efforts, throughout the seventeenth century, to establish the culture and production of silk on a paying basis. However, the lure of profit accruing from the easy tobacco crop, plus the difficulty in obtaining for the Colony skilled silk workers, resulted eventually in the abandonment of the undertaking.

Abundant Supplies for the Colonists

Fearing that their right of assembly, instituted in 1619, would be revoked, the colonists, following the abrogation of the charter of the Virginia Company, opposed the decision of King Charles I, to take over administration of affairs in Virginia, and sent a protest to England, 1625. Nevertheless, facing the inevitable, they acceded to the Royal demands and surrendered the colony to the King. One of the immediate effects of the change in control was a stimulus to trade. So abundant were the supplies brought

17

in by traders, now independent of the requirements formerly placed by the Virginia Company, that the colonists, by 1630, had often become deeply indebted to the English merchants.

An account of a trading voyage to Virginia, a venture in which eight Englishmen joined to send both cargo and indentured servants to the Colony and bring back tobacco, not only conveys an idea of commodities and servants sold for domestic purposes, but projects a picture of life along the estuaries flowing into the Chesapeake Bay, as the ship plied from one plantation wharf to another, selling merchandise and human help, both in demand. The *Tristram and Jane* of London left England in the late summer or early fall of 1636, arriving in Virginia in time for the fall tobacco crop ready for the market in December. Daniel Hopkinson, merchant, was in charge of the cargo, but dying before the ship's return to England, he requested to be "decently" buried at the Kecoughtan (Elizabeth City) Church.

At five or more ports of call, both cargo and servants were disposed of. There were a number of items in the luxury class, such as sack (white wine from southern Europe), strong waters (drink high in alcoholic content), candy oil (olive oil from the island of Crete, originally known as Candia), sugar, both powdered and loaf, shelled almonds (least in demand among the items), marmalade of quinces, conserves of sloes (plums), of roses and barberries, raisins, Sussex cheese, vinegar, and handkerchiefs. Among the more useful items were: 87 pairs of shoes, 12 suits of clothing, nails of various sizes, of which there appeared to be never enough in the Colony, peas and oatmeal. In addition to these, a shallop, a pair of steelyards (scales), and three fowling pieces were disposed of.

The ship stopped first at Kecoughtan (now Hampton), a populous settlement, having been established by the colonists in 1610, and, here, buried Hopkinson and disposed of some of her cargo of seventy-four white persons who were sold as indentured servants. These persons, before embarking from England, had agreed to serve a term of years, usually seven, in the Colony in return for passage, clothes and supplies, to be furnished them at the conclusion of their service. The major portion of help in the colony, at this period, was of this class, although a few Negroes were brought to Virginia by 1619, and approximately a score are listed in the muster of 1625.

Upon departing from Kecoughtan, the ship retraced a portion of her course in the Chesapeake Bay, and entered Back River, on which the Langley Air Force Base and the laboratories for the National Advisory Committee for Aeronautics are now located, and from there entered the Old Poquoson River, later termed the Northwest Branch of Back River. This very populous area was readily accessible to the port of Kecoughtan both by water and by land.

Next, the *Tristram and Jane* discharged cargo and sold servants on the New Poquoson (now Poquoson) River, which flows into the Bay north of Back River. In this latter area, first settled in 1630, patents had been assigned, one including a large acreage to Christopher Calthrope, and it is reasonable to conclude that both commodities and servants were wanted.

From the New Poquoson, the ship sailed across the Chesapeake and traded at Accawmack on the Eastern Shore, and then sailed back towards the mouth of the James River, and entered Chuckatuck Creek and the Nansemond River, where the Gookins, whose father had settled Newport News in 1621, bought two servants. Other ports are not named, but among the purchasers of servants was George Menefie on the James below Jamestown. It is probable that the ship went as far up the River as the mouth of the Appomattox.

Prices paid for the servants were not all the same, and a bonus of fifty acres of land accrued to the planter, if the servant's passage money was added to the purchase price.

Having unloaded the entire cargo, the *Tristram and Jane* took on tobacco for the return voyage, loading 99 hogsheads or a total

19

of 31,800 pounds. In addition, the partners in the shipping enterprise loaded two hogsheads on the *Unity* of Isle of Wight, making a total poundage of 32,350.

The *America* was another of the trading vessels, which made annual voyages to Virginia, between the years 1632 and 1636, and showed a profit, in each of the first three years, of 640 pounds sterling. This was divided among several partners in the enterprise. William Barker was master and part owner of the vessel and made his Virginia headquarters in Norfolk, where brief accounts of the voyages were entered in the Court records, in 1646.

BETTER HOMES

As commodities began to reach Virginia in quantities, tools and building supplies became available, and skilled workers arrived. Thus, homes could be more sturdily built. By 1620, Reverend Richard Buck, who had reached Virginia, 1610, had purchased from William Fairfax the latter's dwelling house located on twelve acres of land in James City. In 1623, William Claiborne was sent to the colony and laid out an area on Jamestown Island known as New Town, where a number of dwellings were erected.

As the colonists had begun to fashion clapboard and wainscoting by 1609, and were using brick made in the Colony by 1612, the houses, built in this newly laid-out area, were far more substantial than the early shelters described. Among those dwelling in New Town, by 1624 were, Richard Stephens, Ralph Hamor, George Menefie, John Chew, Doctor John Pott, Captain John Harvey and Ensign William Spence.

In 1624, John Johnson was ordered by the Court to repair the "late dwelling house" of Spence. References to other houses mentioned are found in the early land patents. Abraham Peirsey, the cape-merchant, directed, in his will dated 1626, that he be buried in his garden, where his new frame house stood. Thomas Dunthorne's house is mentioned, in 1625, and in 1627, Sir

George Yeardley noted, in his will of that date, his dwelling house and other houses at Jamestown.

Since the materials are of record, these recently built homes may be envisioned as having been constructed of hewn timbers, covered with clapboard on the exterior, and wainscoting inside. The foundations and chimneys were of brick, which, while not plentiful, was certainly being supplied within the Colony at the period. Clay from the James River shores and the Chickahominy was available, and reeds from the marshes at hand furnished the necessary straw. It is entirely improbable that bricks were at any time brought from England for building purposes. Cargo space on inbound ships was too valuable and supplies too badly needed to fill ships' holds with bricks, especially when materials for making them were so close at hand.

Similar houses were being built in other areas at the same period. Mrs. Rachel Pollentine's house in Warriscoyack (Isle of Wight) is mentioned in 1628. John Bush had two houses at Kecoughtan by 1618.

Governor Sir John Harvey reported that Richard Kemp, Secretary of the Colony, had the first brick house built in Virginia, in 1636, and at Jamestown. However, Adam Thoroughgood, who was granted land at Lynnhaven in Lower Norfolk County, is said to have begun construction of his brick house there between 1636 and 1640. This house, which has undergone numerous modifications throughout the years, is believed to be the oldest colonial home now standing in Virginia. Originally, it is believed to have been a one story, single-room house with chimneys at both ends. Access to the loft above was by a ladder-like stairway; the dormer windows were a later addition.

A very early house in Virginia, of which there is a clear Court record, is the brick dwelling of the colonial planter Thomas Warren, located on Smith's Fort Plantation, in Surry County. It is sometimes called the Rolfe House, as the land, on which the house was erected, was a gift from the Indian King to Thomas, son of John Rolfe and Pocahontas.

The dwelling-house of Captain Thomas Bernard on Mulberry Island was mentioned in 1641. The Wills family lived in the same area in a brick house during the 1650's, for, in 1659, Henry Jackson bequeathed, to "my widow's eldest son John Wills, the part that belongs to him of my wife's brick house and lands on Mulberry Island."

Before 1627 the first windmill in the colony had been erected and was in operation at Flowerdew Hundred, Governor Yeardley's plantation on the south side of the James River. The more affluent planters like Yeardley, and in keeping with the English customs, maintained homes at the seat of government while operating large plantations on the River not too far distant.

William Peirce, captain of the Governor's guard, had a plantation project on Mulberry Island while he and Mrs. Peirce lived at Jamestown. On a visit to England in 1629, Mrs. Peirce reported, that she had lived for 20 years in the Colony, and from her garden of three or four acres at Jamestown, she had gathered about 100 bushels of figs, and that she could keep a better house in Virginia for three or four hundred pounds a year than in London.

Young Daniel Gookin, probably with his brother John, was living at Newport News in 1633, where their father had established a home called "Marie's Mount," for the Dutch sea-captain Peter deVries recorded that he stopped there over night. The Gookins also maintained a plantation, directly across from Newport News on the Nansemond River, at which point the *Tristram and Jane* called in 1637.

Richard Kingsmill, who patented land at Archer's Hope, James City, in 1626, planted there a pear orchard, and reported later that he had made from fruit gathered there some forty or fifty butts of perry. In addition to his house at Jamestown, George Menefie maintained a plantation, near Archer's Hope Creek, called "Littletown" where he had orchards of apple, pear, cherry and peach trees, and a flower garden especially noted for its rosemary, thyme and marjoram. Captain Brocas of the Council kept an excellent vineyard on his plantation, in Warwick County, patented in 1638. Richard Bennett, of Nansemond River, developed an apple orchard and, in 1648, reported that he had made from it twenty butts of cider.

About 1625, Captain Samuel Mathews moved his seat from the south side of the James River to a location near Blount Point at the mouth of the Warwick River, and across from Mulberry Island, which later was called "Denbigh." He married, a year or two thereafter, the widow of the cape-merchant Abraham Peirsey. A contemporary writer, in 1648, described Mathews' plantation as a miniature village, at the center of which was the manor-house. On surrounding acreage, hemp and flax were sown, and upon being harvested, the flax was spun and woven into cloth in one of the many outbuildings. At a tan-house, eight shoemakers dressed leather and made shoes. There were negro servants, some of whom worked in the fields while others were taught trades. Barley and wheat, grown at "Denbigh," were reported to have been sold at four shillings per bushel. Some of the cattle raised on the place supplied the dairy while others, kept for slaughtering, supplied meat for out-bound vessels. Mathews also kept swine and poultry. Incidentally, Colonel William Cole acquired "Denbigh" from the Mathews family in the latter part of the seventeenth century. In turn, at the beginning of the nineteenth century, descendants of Cole conveyed the original home site and several hundred acres of the plantation to Richard Young, whose descendants still own a portion of it.

"Greenspring," Governor Berkeley's home about three miles inland from Jamestown, was built of brick soon after 1642, to which additions were made at different times; recent excavations show that it was ninety-seven feet, five inches in length by twenty-four feet, nine inches in width. The rooms on the ground floor, overhung by a colonnade, were in single file with an ell on the north front at the west end. Only the foundations of the structure remain. The ever-flowing spring, from which the plantation took its name, is maintained within a brick enclosure.

"Bacon's Castle," in Surry County, built by Arthur Allen soon after his arrival in Virginia about 1650, passed to his son, Speaker of the House of Burgesses, from whom it was seized by Bacon's followers, 1676, and garrisoned by sympathizers under William Rookings. Bacon is not known to have visited the house, although, since its eventful occupation by his followers, the early Allen home has been known by his name. The cluster chimney is a unique feature of its architecture, as is the gabled end. The bricks were laid in English bond.

Of the typical frame homes of the seventeenth century, occupied by the average family, not one remains, which can be dated with authority. However, from extant descriptions, it is known that these modest homes for the most part were one-story structures, with a loft above, to which there was access by means of a ladder-like stairway. Dormer windows, added in the eighteenth century to some of the homes, made of the loft a half-story, providing for more comfortable sleeping quarters for the family. There were chimneys at both ends of these early homes, and meals were prepared on the open hearth of the larger fireplace. The early homes apparently had no partitions, but by the middle of the century, some were divided by one partition on the lower floor. Cellars were not practical in the low-lying areas, for in wet weather the water-table is level with the ground. Inland, for the better homes, in the last half of the century, there were cellars, though some of the more modest structures merely had unbricked excavations below for storage purposes. The size of the modest homes varied, in length, between thirty and forty feet and, in width, between eighteen and twenty feet. In 1679, Major Thomas Chamberlaine, of Henrico, contracted for a frame house forty by twenty feet without a cellar. In 1686, Benjamin Branch's brothers built for him "a home twenty feet long" on the family plantation "Kingsland" in Henrico.

THE FOREST PRIMEVAL

When the English transported themselves or were transported to Virginia, they brought with them as much of England as possible in their manners, their customs, their pride in family and race, their laws and their possessions. With something of nostalgia for home, they often named their plantations for the family estates in England, and the locales, in which they settled, for the shires or the communities near their old world homes. They did not seek to create a new race, as did the Spanish in settling Louisiana who designated themselves *Criollo*, but to remain Englishmen in the new world. To this end they were willing to struggle and overcome a wilderness. In so doing, they sharpened their native acumen, awakened their inherent resourcefulness, and eventually in the eighteenth century, established themselves as a free and independent people.

Their manner of living in Virginia was determined, not so much by design, as by force of circumstances. Available land and tobacco were determining factors in developing large plantations along the main waterways and small plantations in the hinterlands. Self-sufficiency was concomitant with their way of life.

Although, in several acts of the Assembly, the first in 1680, efforts were made by authorities to create towns, establish central warehouses, and so bring the people together, such attempts met with only partial success. Towns that were projected, in 1680, in expectation of developing centers of population, were difficult to promote. Once started, they languished, as did Warwicktown in one of the eight original shires. Except for its ports of entry, such as Jamestown, Norfolk and Kecoughtan, Virginia in the seventeenth century was not adapted to urban living.

Upon arrival in Virginia, the colonists faced a vast forest.

25

Before them in the April sunshine was a massive wall of shimmering green in the stately pines, cedars and holly, intermingled with the freshly unfolded leaves of the venerable oak, walnut, hickory and beech. There were no grassy plains, no open fields, save the garden plots of small tribes of Indians. Clearing the land, in itself, was a tremendous task.

The choice acreage ever in demand by the colonists was, of course, the open land found in and near the Indian villages. Many a land patent later embraced an Indian field. The Company lands in Elizabeth City were the fertile fields of the Kecoughtan Indians, who had been driven from their habitations there, in 1610, after the murder of a colonist, Humphrey Blount. Following the massacre of 1622, the natives were relentlessly driven from their villages and fields—the Warriscoyacks, the Nansemonds, the Chickahominies and in 1630, the Chiskiackes. Then, the white men took over their areas of cleared land.

However, these fields were but small open spaces required by the Englishmen who arrived in increasing numbers. There was a constant operation, in the seventeenth century, of clearing and planting new lands. As help in the white indentured servants was never very plentiful, the planters, finally resorted to an available supply of Negro labor, being peddled along the coast of the Americas, and landed wherever the slaveships could gain entry.

The muster of 1625 shows that many goats had been brought to the Colony by that time. Multiplying, they provided able assistance during the early seventeenth century in thoroughly clearing away the undergrowth, preparatory to cutting down trees and grubbing stumps. Joseph Ham, in the colony by 1633, resorted to these omnivorous quadrupeds in clearing his land. He lived in the New Poquoson area where growth of all kinds is lush. The region, which has its name from the Indian term for lowlands, had afforded the Kecoughtan Indians a rich hunting-ground. Midst tall pines, oak, walnut, cedar, wild cherry,

26

locust, swamp willow, holly, myrtle and persimmon, entangled with grape vines, reaching the tops of trees, and Virginia creeper, game found a haven. Deer, bears, rabbits, squirrel, opossum, racoon, foxes, weasels, mink, otter and muskrat were sheltered in the thickets and adjacent swamps, while wild ducks and geese made of the marshes, bordering the waterways, a rendezvous for days and weeks on their flights southward. The Bay at hand, and its estuaries, abounded in trout, hogfish, rock, shad, sturgeon and other edible species in season, not to speak of soft-shell crabs, hard-shell crabs, turtles, terrapin, clams and oysters.

Here was food in plenty, but to clear the land for a crop posed a problem to Joseph Ham. He had married a widow with two young children and the family had one servant only—a maid. The heavy work fell to him, but not all of it, for he turned fifty-one goats into the thickets to feast upon the vines and undergrowth. When he died, in 1638, he bequeathed his herd of goats to his stepchildren and to his wife. Although he left other possessions, including a feather bed, two blankets, a rug, a bolster, a warming-pan, a parcel of pewter, three iron pots, two brass kettles, a brass basin, a copper kettle, three pairs of sheets, one dozen napkins, a table-cloth, a looking-glass, a chest, ten barrels of corn and three shoats, along with his plantation, yet the goats had been his first thought. He carefully designated thirty for his stepchildren and twenty-one for his wife. The present may measure the worth of the goats in the early seventeenth century by this scrupulous legacy.

THE INDEPENDENT PLANTER

In establishing the colony, the Virginia Company had projected the idea that the people who settled the land would, in a short time, be able to supply their daily needs. In addition, they would ship to England raw materials needed there, and absorb in return articles produced by the English craftsmen, and such imports from foreign lands as were surplus in England. Thus,

27

a brisk trade was anticipated, and did develop, but not in the direction forecast in the beginning.

As the forests were rapidly being depleted in England, wood and wood products were among the greatest needs. Accordingly, report was made in 1624, that, by 1608 and 1609, such woods as cedar, cypress and black walnut had been exported from the Colony, and both clapboard and wainscoting, fashioned in Virginia, had been sent to the Mother Country, along with soap ashes, yielding the necessary potash, an ingredient for soap-making scarce in England. In addition, pitch, tar, iron ore, sturgeon and glass were exported and sassafras, growing wild in Virginia, was in demand in England for tea making. Ere long, of course, the colonists found that tobacco was a lucrative crop, and put their time, attention and efforts in developing a grade of tobacco, which would bring a good price. Inspection before exportation helped in maintaining the standard.

However, in cultivating tobacco, the Virginia planter also promoted assiduously a program of self-sufficiency for his plantation, so that what was needed in daily living was at hand or could be had from a neighbor. Practically every plantation, both large and small, had livestock and produced milk and butter. Sufficient quantities of corn, barley and wheat were grown to supply year-around needs. Very soon the Englishmen abandoned the Indian method of pounding grain into meal for bread-making and established mills on the fresh-water courses and on tidal waters where the dammed streams and the tide furnished water-power. Mill stones were among early shipments to the colony and locations of some of these seventeenth-century mills remain landmarks in Virginia today. Denbigh, on Waters Creek in Warwick County, Chuckatuck in Nansemond, and the headwaters of the Poquoson in York County are among the sites of early mills. John Bates of Skimeno in Upper York County, a large land owner, operated two mills, one on his plantation called "Pease Hill creek mill" and the other, "Okenneck," a water-grist-mill.

Brandy for family use often was distilled on the plantation. While Philip Fisher of the Eastern Shore bequeathed both his mill and his still to his son Thomas, he directed that his son John should have the use of both, the mill to grind his corn and the still "to still his own drink." Beer was made from malt, and cider was produced from apples grown on the plantations.

The remains of an icehouse uncovered during excavations at Jamestown, and dated about the middle of the seventeenth century, is evidence that the colonists cut ice from the ponds nearby, during a freeze, and stored it for use in summer. These cylindrical structures, usually of brick, erected in a shady spot and reinforced at the base with the cooling earth, were packed ten, fifteen or more feet deep with ice, depending on the supply available. In between the layers, straw and reeds were laid, and the arrangement in general preserved the ice even into the very warm months.

Thomas Cocke, of "Pickthorn Farm" and "Malvern Hill," carried on enterprises established by his father, operating at the latter a flour mill, tanneries and looms for making both woolens and linen. For a specimen of linen five ells in length and three-fourths of a yard wide of the first quality, he received an award, in 1695, of 800 pounds of tobacco, offered by the Assembly in 1692. Both Virginia-made stockings and Virginia-made cloth are listed in the Bridger inventory of 1686.

A pottery kiln, uncovered at "Greenspring," and in operation prior to 1675, shows the interest of the Virginia Governor in having earthenware fashioned in the colony for domestic uses. Morgan Jones of Westmoreland County is mentioned as a "potter" in 1674. At the same time, Joseph Copeland of Chuckatuck, in Nansemond County, was fashioning pewter. The handle of a spoon bearing the hallmark of this earliest American pewterer, of whom there is a record, is extant and may be seen at the museum at Jamestown.

Some of the earliest of the colonists were skilled in boatbuilding, the shipwrecked passengers on the *Seaventure* having constructed, on the Bermuda Islands in 1609, two pinnaces in which they sailed the 700 miles to Virginia in 1610. The Hansfords maintained a boatyard on Felgate's Creek in York County, where they both built and repaired small vessels. On 17 November 1675, John Allen, Augustine Kneaton and William Hobson of Northumberland County agreed to build a sloop of twenty-four feet by the keel for Andrew Pettigrew and deliver it to his plantation, the sloop to be able "to floor [lay flat] nine hogsheads complete."

These brief mentions by no means complete the story of the independent Virginia planter, who acquired the luxuries shipped from England as the proceeds from his tobacco crop permitted, but who generally had at hand the necessities of life regardless of the times.

PART II

THE VIRGINIA PLANTERS AND THEIR MANNER OF LIVING

A YOUNGER SON IN VIRGINIA

The progress, from the status of a younger son in England, to that of a landed proprietor in Virginia, is illustrated in the typical case of Christopher Calthrope, third son of Christopher Calthrope Esq. of Blakeney, Norfolk, England. The seniority of two brothers was a limitation upon opportunity for him in England. As a youth of sixteen years of age he was sent to Virginia, in 1622, in company with Lieutenant Thomas Purefoy, the latter named later Commander of Elizabeth City Corporation.

Young Calthrope had been well supplied by his family before leaving England, even bringing with him a quantity of "good liquor" which, while it lasted, added considerably to his popularity. In the name of the family attorney, the young man shortly was assigned land on Waters Creek, in the area now the site of the Mariners Museum of Warwick. In 1628, he also owned land in a choice area near Fort Henry and adjacent to Lieutenant Purefoy in Elizabeth City.

These tracts, however, provided but small plantations, and so when the area along the York River was opened for settlement in 1630, Christopher Calthrope sought land available in large tracts in the adjacent territory, patenting some 1200 acres on the New Poquoson (now Poquoson) River, which flows into the Chesapeake Bay just beyond the mouth of the York. He called his new plantation "Thropland" after the family estate in England. By 1635, a church had been built on his land and New Poquoson Parish (later Charles Parish) was established, the records of which are the earliest extant Parish records in

31

Virginia. As the Parish then embraced the areas on the west side of the river, the Chismans and other families who had settled on Chisman's Creek, sailed over in their sloops or came in their shallops, to worship there on Sundays.

Captain Christopher Calthrope, the Virginia planter, served both York and Elizabeth City in the House of Burgesses during the period, 1644-1660, and also was one of the Commissioners for York County. He was replaced in the latter office, 1661, since he had gone *Southward*, the designation then for the area, which lay on the southern border of Virginia and the northern boundary of the present state of North Carolina. Vast tracts of land were available there, and Calthrope, still land hungry, acquired acreage in the Nottoway region, on which his great grandson was living in 1756.

Shortly after Calthrope's demise, his widow Anne petitioned the York County Court to grant her administration of his estate, and on 24 April, 1662, she gave bond with very good security in return for her appointment. Six months later the inventory estimated the estate, with several items not then accounted for, at "30,480 pounds of tobacco and casks." The widow, a son and three daughters shared in the estate, which not only included land in York and at the *Southward*, but possessions in a considerable number.

Both tobacco and corn were raised on the Calthrope land, hives of bees were kept, and a dairy was in operation. To aid the family enterprise there were nine indentured servants, one of whom, Thomas Ragg, later became the husband of Elinor Calthrope.

Four draught oxen did the hauling on the low-lying plantation. Also there were six steers, thirteen milch cows, five heifers, four yearlings and seven calves, the cows obviously supplying the dairy equipped with ten milk trays, a tub and earthenware pan. Three sows, two barrows and four shoats completed the list of livestock.

All other possessions are listed in the "outer room, the chamber and the shedd." These three areas constituted the Calthrope home. In the chamber where the family apparently lived and slept, there were two feather beds, with the usual appurtenances of bolsters, sheets, blankets, valances and curtains, and also a couch bed and a couch. In the outer room, apparently a store-room, there was, in accordance with the practice of planters to keep a supply of materials on hand, a quantity of piece-goods in dowlas, lockram, dimity, coarse Holland, fine Holland and tufted Holland, osnaburg and kersey, and seventeen ells (45 inches in English measure and 27 inches in Dutch measure) of sheeting, as well as yarn stockings. A limited supply of colored calico, East Indian stuff and Norway stuff are evidence that the English merchantmen, tramping to all parts of the world, brought some of their cargoes from remote areas to Virginia.

Cooking was carried on in the shed, probably a thinly enclosed area, equipped with a large fireplace and attached to the house. Here, there were andirons, racks, a spit, hooks and bellows. Utensils for preparing food included an iron pot, a gridiron, frying-pan, dripping-pan, two brass kettles, a skimmer, a mortar and pestle, and a grater. Pewter-ware and a supply of three dozen napkins and six tablecloths made meals something of an occasion for the family.

Evidently, the Calthrope family had little fear of enemies in their area, from which the Indians had previously been driven away, for they owned but one gun and that was "unfixt," that is, not equipped with a firing mechanism.

James Calthrope, only son of Christopher, inherited his father's plantation, served as Justice of York County and, in his will, proved 1690, bequeathed land to New Poquoson Parish, which evidently was that upon which the church had originally been erected.

The fourth generation of Calthropes in Virginia maintained title to a portion of the York County grant, more than a century and a quarter, after the progenitor of the family came to the colonies. Thus, did the Englishmen reach out across the seas, and plant branches of their families to carry on in the English tradition in the new world.

ROYALISTS IN VIRGINIA

By 1644, conditions in England had become difficult because of the Civil Wars. In a correspondence with Daniel Llewellyn of Charles City, William Hallom of England wrote: "if these times hold long amongst us we must all faine come to Virginia."

The message sent by Hallom was prophetic, for by 1650, many well-to-do Englishmen, loyal to the Crown, fled to Virginia to escape the wrath of Cromwell's men. Some were so deeply involved politically that they assumed aliases. This was the case of Captain Francis Dade, who, until the Restoration, was known in Virginia as Major John Smith. Many, who came to Virginia during this period, remained. Mrs. Anne Gorsuch, whose husband, a Royalist, was pursued and killed in England, brought seven of her children to Virginia, but on returning to see to her affairs there, died. The children remained and established families in Virginia and Maryland. Daniel Horsmanden later returned to England and died there; however, his daughter Ursula married, as her second husband, William Byrd I and established the well-known Virginia family of that name.

Also, representative of the Royalists who migrated to Virginia was Colonel Joseph Bridger of Isle of Wight County. The date of his coming is unknown, but he appeared in the records as a member of the House of Burgesses, 1657; thus, apparently, he had been in the county several years prior to that time. His tombstone, uncovered at the site of his home plantation, "White Marsh," was removed in the late nineteenth century and placed in the chancel of the Old Brick Church (St. Luke's) in the county.

Colonel Bridger established in Isle of Wight a large mercantile business, trading Virginia tobacco for commodities needed by the colonists. In addition, on several plantations, aggregating in total over 12000 acres, he raised tobacco and cattle, the latter apparently to supply ships departing for England. As a successful business man he shortly rose to prominence in the colony; he was a member of the Commission to adjust the boundary between Maryland and Virginia, 1664, a member of the Council, 1675, and sat on Governor Berkeley's court at "Greenspring," which condemned to death leaders of Bacon's Rebellion. In 1680, he was commander-in-chief of the militia of Isle of Wight, Surry, Lower Norfolk and Upper Norfolk (Nansemond) Counties, with the title of Major General. Evidently, he maintained a close association with Governor Berkeley, for he was a witness to the latter's will, 2 May 1676. His own will, dated 3 August 1683, with a codicil attached less than two months later, together with the inventory of his extensive estate, taken in 1686, provides interesting information as to the manner of living of the Virginia merchant and planter of the latter half of the seventeenth century.

In the settlement, Colonel Bridger's holdings were shared by his wife Hester (Pitt) and six of his seven children. The eldest son was excluded from his inheritance as Colonel Bridger, evidently a martinet with his family as well as in his official capacity, added in the codicil a directive cutting him off with 2000 pounds of tobacco because Joseph Jr. had been disobedient to him and had gone out in "diverse ways." In friendly suits with his brothers, after his father's death, the disinherited son gained possession of a large portion of his rightful heritage.

The family lived on the 850 acre plantation which Colonel Bridger had purchased from Captain Upton. There was on the place a brick house when the Bridger inventory was taken. There were four rooms on the first floor, including the children's chamber and the dining room, with two rooms in an upper story. Also a "new house" is listed in which there were the hall, the parlor and the lower chamber on the first floor, and on the upper floor three rooms and a "gallery" (hall). All rooms and the halls in both houses were fully furnished. In the cellar beneath the new house the family supply of drink was kept. The kitchen with two additional chambers was probably separate from the house.

The mercantile business was carried on from a store, with an outer room, a supply room in the rear and a storeroom above. Also, there was a brick store, probably a warehouse, with storage space above. Merchandise brought from England was unloaded at the landing, where an unusual item of 800 "painting tiles" is listed. These imported tiles became popular, in the latter part of the century, for facing fireplaces and other uses.

A sloop, with a capacity of twenty-eight hogsheads, equipped with "furniture, sails, rigging and ground tackle" is accounted for in the inventory. Tobacco was picked up at the planters' wharfs, as goods shipped from England, through the Bridger agents, Micajah Perry and Thomas Lane, were delivered on the sloop.

Livestock was kept at pasture at the home plantation, at John Cahan's and at "Curowoak," the latter an 8000 acre grant. There were fifty-four head of cattle, and seven calves, these probably for butchering, thirteen cows and five yearlings for dairy supplies; eight oxen were used for heavy hauling, and besides there were nine steers and four bulls. Of old hogs, young hogs, sows, shoats and pigs there were fifty-four and, in addition, seven sheep and fourteen horses.

Colonel Bridger owned 490 ounces of plate (silver) and had on hand, at the time of his death, Spanish money valued at sixty pounds and English money valued at forty-two pounds ten shillings.

In addition to these holdings, obligations due the merchant both in money and tobacco, are recorded, showing the extent of the business he carried on with the planters, who lived for the most part on the James River and its estuaries. Among those indebted to the Bridger estate were Colonel William Byrd for twelve pounds, John Pleasants for five pounds, John Champion for 958 pounds of tobacco, Thomas Pitt for 2000 pounds of tobacco and Colonel Christopher Wormeley in a bill of exchange amounting to eight pounds. Besides, Perry and Lane in London held bills of exchange to Bridger's credit amounting to 654 pounds.

Four indentured servants, with existing terms of service, and thirteen Negroes including two small children, are listed by name in the inventory. A Negro, obviously from the West Indies, was called "Monsieur."

The enumeration of items in the two houses are of interest, as they show the more elaborate type of furnishings, that began to flow into the colony, after the middle of the century. The houses were heated as customary in the seventeenth century by fireplaces, for numerous andirons, either brass or iron, are listed together with tongs and fire-shovels. Numerous candlesticks, some of brass, some of wire and others of silver, illuminated the rooms in the evening. Chairs, rare in the early part of the century, were not scarce by 1686, for they are mentioned as caned, of leather, or covered either with serge or turkey-work, as were several couches. Tables of various sizes, a great looking-glass, a number of chests, several chests of drawers, and pictures were among the furnishings.

The beds were of the usual two types—the bedstead with feather-bedding, bolster and pillows being the more elegant, while the less important folks were assigned flock beds. Both types had curtains and valances, were supplied with blankets and sheets, the latter, either of canvas or Holland, and there were several quilts. The use of rugs mentioned is undetermined, for these often served as covering, or were hung on the walls to keep out the drafts. However, there was a carpet in the "great hall" of the new house, where also stood a clock, and unusual items as, three pairs of steelyards (scales).

There was a plentiful supply of table-linen in cloths and napkins of various qualities, the diaper linen (damask) being the best. The tableware for the most part was of pewter, some four dozen plates being listed, together with porringer, chafing-dish, fish-plates and pie-plates. Among the silver was a punch bowl, candlesticks, serving dish, several spoons and the cover of a tobacco box.

The family was one of some learning for a parcel of books is listed; and evidently Colonel Bridger was interested in the mysteries of the times, for a book on *Witchcraft* and another on *Astrology* are mentioned particularly.

In addition to the planter's usual possession of arms for family protection, in a capacity of high ranking officer of the militia, Colonel Bridger had on hand several guns, a case of pistols and holsters, and a pair of pocket pistols, a hanger (type of cutlass), three rapiers, one with a silver hilt, and ammunition.

Among the interesting items in his possession were a parcel of Virginia-made cloth and fourteen pairs of Virginia stockings. As these were in the home, it is possible that they were made on the plantation.

The size of some of the kitchen utensils and equipment point to a kitchen, with a very large fireplace, occupying an end of the room, where all food was prepared and cooked over the burning coals of a plentiful supply of wood. There were two great copper kettles weighing sixty-one pounds and forty pounds respectively, a brass kettle weighing fifty pounds, and two great andirons weighing 105 pounds, two iron pots weighing forty pounds each, four pot hooks, a heavy mall, three spits and skillets of several sizes. In the room adjoining the kitchen the milk was cared for, as there were eleven milk-pans, an "earthen" pan and three "earthen" butter-pots.

In the cellar was the gentleman's supply of drink, cider for family use, a cask of brandy, a cask of old whiskey, and a malt-mill listed as worn out.

While it is not practicable to mention here all of the goods

38

carried in the store and the storehouse, certain of the items are of special interest, such as materials used for wearing apparel of the period, accessories of dress, utensils and agricultural tools available in Virginia. About twenty different materials of varying qualities were imported from England. They were woven for the most part of flax, hemp or wool, or combinations, with some cotton, not generally in use, but available in a few materials.

Osnaburg, a coarse, heavy linen suitable for work clothes, or for sails, was available in quantities, in brown, for the former and white, for the latter; canvas, a closely woven cloth, of hemp or flax, was used for various purposes and appears to have been of different weights, for often canvas sheets are mentioned, which undoubtedly were of the lighter grade; dowlas, very much in use in the Colony, was a coarse linen made in the north of England and in Scotland, and today replaced in use by calico. Various weights of serge were listed, similar, no doubt, to the serge the present knows, for it was used for suits, coats and dresses. Linsey, a coarse cloth, was made of linen and wool, or occasionally of cotton and wool; kersey, a knit woolen cloth, usually coarse and ribbed, manufactured in England as early as the thirteenth century, was especially for hose; lockram was a sort of a coarse linen or hempen cloth, and penniston, a coarse woolen frieze. Shalloon, a woolen fabric of twill weave was used chiefly for linings; fustian was a cotton and linen cloth, and diaper linen was woven of flax with a raised figure such as in damask, and used chiefly for table-linen.

In addition, the Bridger store had on its shelves, colored calico, a small amount of flannel, some broadcloth, and a small parcel of silk valued at one pound. There was also thread in brown and other colors, knitting-needles, pins, horn-combs, combs made of ivory and knives of various descriptions. For trimming garments, there was guimpe, colored tape, Holland tape and Hamburg, the latter an embroidered edging, buttons, some silk covered. Oth-

39

er items included skeins of twine, whalebone, scissors, and 132 pounds of soap.

Among the building supplies were quantities of nails of all sizes, which ever seemed to be in great demand in the Colony. For the field, there were narrow hoes and weeding-hoes, axes of different types, as well as a whipsaw.

For home furnishings, are listed such items as feather bedticks and bolsters, Irish bedticks, plain rugs, matting rugs, the latter showing importations from the Orient to England and thence to the Colony. Also, there were blankets, curtains and valances for tester beds, counterpanes of serge, table-knives with white handles, black handles, and ivory handles; in pewter, the store offered porringers, plates, serving-dishes and candlesticks. Among supplies, in addition to soap and twine, there were fifty-five bushels of salt and a barrel of coarse sugar.

The colonists, used to their drink, found an ever-flowing cheap supply from the West Indies in rum, distilled there from molasses produced from sugar cane. This drink was stocked especially for the servants in the Colony. The Bridger store had on hand six barrels and one hogshead of rum, the entire contents being approximately two hundred and fifty-five gallons. In addition, there had been laid aside "for Colonel Powell's hands" sixty-five gallons of rum.

In wearing apparel, the store was stocked with shoes for men, women and boys, hose for men and women, hats at various prices, bodices for women, "plaines" for men and boys and "falls" for men and boys.

The little pest, the moth, had made its appearance in Virginia, for in goods accounted for, are four pairs of moth-eaten hose and a piece of moth-eaten kersey.

No firearms are listed in the salable goods on hand but 106 pounds of shot are valued at 12s 6d.

Urban folks, coming to Virginia in the early twentieth century, and visiting rural areas, were wont to comment upon the inevitable horse-collars and harness that usually held a prominent place in the cluttered country store. They were no less indispensable to travel over the dirt roads of that time than were the harness accessories in the Bridger store, such as snaffles and check-bits, stirrup-leathers, halters and girths. While, as hereafter mentioned, the waterways in Virginia served as open travel routes, the use of the horse was more or less general by the latter part of the century, at least among the well-to-do, for riding about the plantation, for visiting, and for sport in racing. As noted, Colonel Bridger owned fourteen horses.

The shares in the estate of Colonel Bridger's three married daughters were claimed by their husbands and are recorded by items. It is of interest to note that Thomas Godwin, husband of Martha Bridger, was speaker of the House of Burgesses, in 1676, that Thomas Lear, who married Elizabeth Bridger, was a prominent planter of Nansemond County, and Richard Tibboth, husband of Mary Bridger, was master of the ship *Anne and Mary*, which plied between England and "James River in Virginia."

THE STATUS OF WOMEN

Notwithstanding the declaration by Virginia's first representative legislative Assembly in session at Jamestown, 30 July 1619, that "in a new plantation it is not known which be the most necessary, man or woman," the plantation representatives saw fit to extend to the married women only one benefit for having come to the colony, and that was the continuation of the bonus of fifty acres of land in control of their husbands. A married woman in the Colony had no title whatsover to possessions during her husband's lifetime. She could not hold land in her name; any bequest from the estate of her parents became her husband's property, and the receipt of it was acknowledged in Court by him. Colonel Joseph Bridger sought through terms in his will, dated 1683, to prevent the husband of his daughter Martha from coming into possession of her inheritance, stipulating that his bequest to her was for her sole use and, should her husband desire to dispose of it, then, the inheritance should not come into his hands but should remain under control of the executrix. Nevertheless, Thomas Godwin signed a receipt for his wife's portion, according to law, and despite the Colonel's last wishes, it became his sole possession.

If a woman married a second or third time, land and possessions held in her name, during her widowhood, immediately became the property of the next husband. For that reason, women, on contemplating a second marriage, and wishing the children by a former husband to have the benefit of their father's holdings, either gave them title to the possessions, just prior to the intended marriage, or exacted from the prospective husband an agreement to give the child or children possession of their rightful inheritance, upon arriving at age. This agreement was duly recorded in the court records.

Now and then, a marriage agreement was so drawn, that the prospective husband's plantation was assured to his intended bride and her heirs, and could therefore never come into possession of a second wife or her heirs. A most careful legal maneuvering to this end is recorded in a marriage agreement, 1652, between Frances Culpeper and Captain Samuel Stephens. On the eve of marriage, the intended groom conveyed his 1350 acre plantation, "Bolthrope" on the Warwick River, in trust to Warham Horsmanden and George Hunt, who then according to agreement, reconveyed the land to Stephens during his lifetime. At his death, according to the terms stipulated, Frances (Culpeper) Stephens his wife came into sole possession.

About the same time, 1651, John Chew of York County, was able to have drawn a less exacting contract on the eve of his second marriage. While he agreed to give, to his prospective bride Mrs. Rachel Constable, the plantation upon which he then lived, a provision was inserted that should she predecease him without heirs, the contract was void. A marriage contract drawn, 1667, between John Savage of the Eastern Shore and his intended second wife Mary Robins, stipulated that his "home plantation at the bottom of the neck" should go to her heirs.

As stated, provision for children of a first husband were often a part of the marriage agreement. Mrs. Sarah Fleete exacted from Colonel John Walker, before the nuptials, a pledge that he would give to her daughter by a first marriage, 400 pounds of lawful money of England within the expiration of six months, or at Mary Burden's arrival at the age of sixteen years. When Mrs. Elizabeth Sheppard of Surry County agreed to a marriage with Thomas Warren, the contract, duly recorded, was very specific. Warren was to have full control of her first husband's estate, with certain exceptions of livestock to be given to Mrs. Sheppard's children. Her stepchildren, as provided in the contract, were to have their full inheritances left them by their father.

Mrs. Elizabeth Mihill, widow of Edward Mihill of New Poquoson (later Charles) Parish, was much less generous with her prospective bridegroom in a contract drawn, 1661. Being about to marry William Hay, Gentleman, of the same Parish, Mrs. Mihill placed everything she owned in the hands of her kin, forever barring the third husband from coming into possession of the holdings of the two prior spouses. She deeded to her son Robert Sheild, by her first husband, all the land and buildings left to her by her second husband, and further directed that should her son leave no heirs, then, her brother Arthur Bray of London should have the estate. The only concession which she made to her prospective third husband was an agreement that he should have one acre of land, but the condition of this gift was that he grind for her son Robert, toll free, 100 bushels weekly, and allow her son also the use of the timber on the land. In addition, she gave her cattle and a servant to her son, and assigned gifts of her possessions to other relatives. To these unusual terms, William Hay, evidently an ardent suitor in pursuit of the widow, agreed, and upon her marriage to him shortly thereafter, he dutifully came into Court and acknowledged his assent to the terms of the settlement.

As the death rate in Virginia in the seventeenth century was high, remarriages were frequent, both on the part of the men and the women. Colonel Thomas Swann of Surry County had five wives as did Major Joseph Croshaw of York County. Women frequently married three or four times. Upon the decease of their husbands, they often found themselves in possession of large isolated plantations. Often, there were indentured white servants, some negroes, and generally a number of children under age. How to manage alone, and thus encumbered, was the problem, and they solved it frequently by marrying shortly a neighbor. He, probably a widower, took charge of the first husband's holdings, settled the involved estate, and gave much needed protection to the woman in a sparsely settled area. This was the case with Mrs. Elizabeth Hansford of York County, who, at the death of her husband, faced the task of managing a plantation, seeing to cultivation of the land, disposing of his maritime interests, and at the same time, seeing to the interests of seven children. Overwhelmed with possessions, and already having her hands full with her domestic affairs, she knew not where to turn for a solution except to a second husband. Ere long, she married the York County merchant Edward Lockey, who at once began the settlement of her late husband's estate, entering an inventory in York County Court records, 1667.

In the very early period of the colony, the grief of the widow was of short duration, for a suitor usually stood at her doorstep almost as the funeral procession ended. The most generally known, of such incidents, was the pursuit of Cicely Jordan, upon the death of her husband Samuel. Within two days Reverend Greville Pooley pressed his suit. The widow tentatively agreeing, but evidently pregnant with the unborn child of her deceased husband, insisted that she would marry no man until she was "delivered." In the meantime, William Farrar, named administra-

44

A Lady of Fashion

Garbed in a costume typical of the early seventeenth century a lady of fashion displays jewels similar to those brought to Virginia by well-to-do merchants.

Photo by Thomas L. Williams through courtesy of the Jamestown Corporation, Inc.

A Gay Mood

A young girl displays a seventeenth-century costume with full skirt, cylindrical bodice and falling band (large loose collar).

A Virginia artisan, in the costume of the early seventeenth century, views a woodland scene in the Jamestown area.

Wash-day in the Seventeenth Century

The women soak the clothes in hot water dipped from the nearby kettle heated over the open fire, beat out the grime with paddles, rinse the articles in the shallow stream and hang them out to dry.

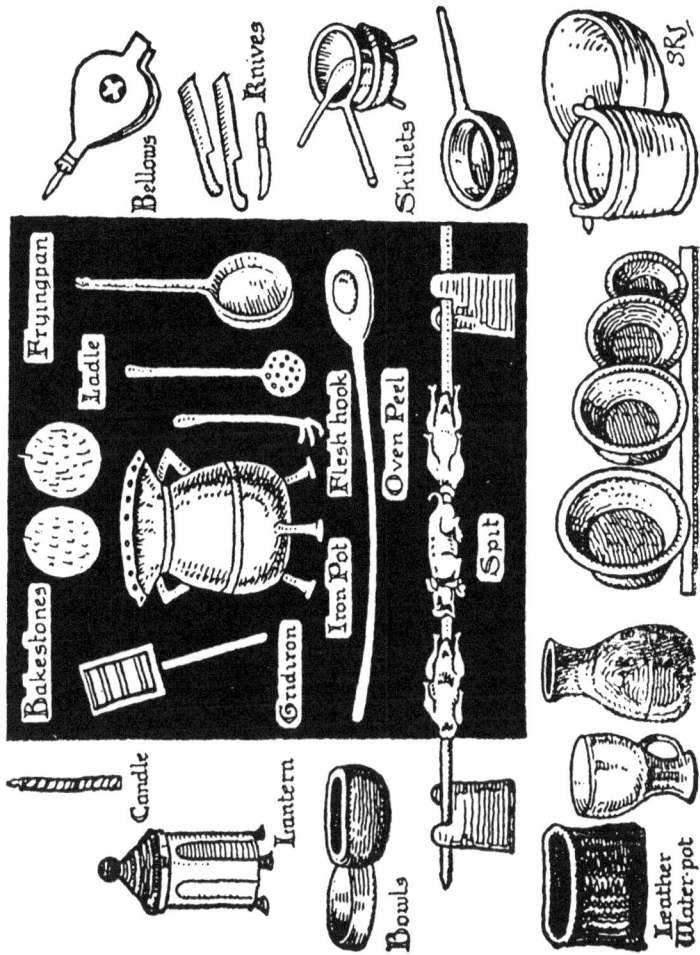

Seventeenth-Century Kitchen and Cooking Utensils

Bellows

Knives

Skillets

Fryingpan

Ladle

Flesh hook

Oven Peel

Spit

Iron Pot

Bakestones

Gridiron

Candle

Lantern

Bowls

Leather Water-pot

Courtesy of the artist, Sydney R. Jones from *Old English Household Life* by Jekyll and Jones, published by B. T. Batsford, Ltd., London.

Photo by Thomas L. Williams

Photo of a group in the U. S. National Museum, Washington, D. C.

Captain John Smith and companions trading with the Indians in Virginia, 1607
The colonists seek corn and furs from the natives in exchange for beads, trinkets, utensils and cloth.

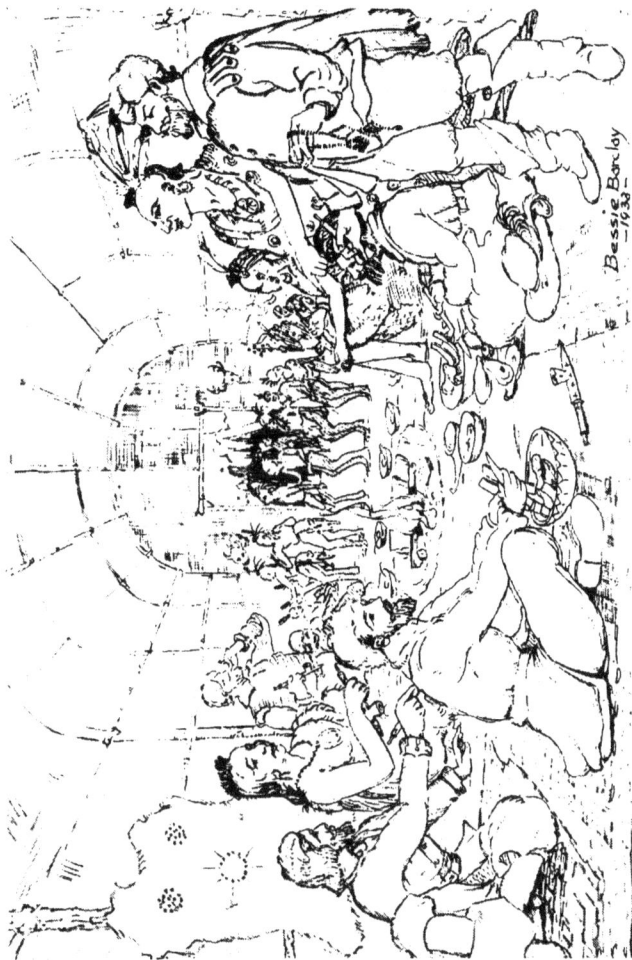

Drawing by the late Bessie Barclay, based on a study of the original John White drawings made in 1585 and now in the British Museum. Through courtesy of the *Daily Press*. Newport News.

Christmas at Kecoughtan 1608

A group of colonists from Jamestown bound for Powhatan's seat on the York River put in at Kecoughtan after encountering adverse weather. There they spent Christmas with the Indians who entertained them in the native arched bark-house with feasting and a tribal dance.

Photo by Flournoy, Virginia State Chamber of Commerce

Upper Weyanoke—Charles City County

Built on the north bank of the James River about the middle of the seventeenth century, the center building of "Upper Weyanoke" originally served also as a stronghold against Indian assault. The wings attached to the dwelling are modern additions.

Early Dining Table

Wainscot Chair

Though the first tables in the Colony were boards laid on trestles, the above shows the adaptation of supports for permanent placing of this article in the household.

While stools and benches were commonly used for seats in the early seventeenth century, a wainscot chair as shown above was in use at Jamestown before 1623.

Windsor Castle—Isle of Wight County

This home is located on a portion of the original grant of 1450 acres to Arthur Smith I, who came to the Colony in 1622. The town of Smithfield was laid out in 1752 by his great-grandson Arthur Smith IV, to whom the General Assembly granted permission to partition off seventy-five acres of his entailed estate.

Photo by Flournoy, Virginia State Chamber of Commerce

Rosegill—Middlesex County

The first Ralph Wormeley, who died in 1651, at the early age of thirty-one, cordially welcomed refugee royalists to Rosegill. Sir Henry Chicheley, Deputy Governor, made his home at Rosegill and died here Dec. 1, 1682. In 1686, the second Ralph Wormeley was host to the Frenchman Monsieur Durand of Dauphiné, who sought in the Colony a haven for the Huguenots, his forlorn compatriots.

Four Mile Tree—Surry County

A seventeenth-century home was the basis for this present structure located on a portion of a 2250 acre grant to Henry Browne in 1637. The estate remained in the family for two hundred years. In the adjacent graveyard may be seen the oldest tomb in Virginia with a legible inscription, that of Alice (Miles) Jordan, who died in 1650.

Adam Thoroughgood House—Princess Anne County

This house, considerably altered, an example of early seventeenth-century architecture, located in that part of Lower Norfolk County which became Princess Anne in 1691, was built by Adam Thoroughgood on land patented by him, 1635. The dormer windows are a later addition.

Warren House—Surry County

Thomas Warren's "fifty foot brick house" on Smith's Fort Plantation was mentioned in a deposition recorded in Surry County as having been, in 1654, "recently completed." The structure now standing is a version of the original house, which apparently was rebuilt about the end of the seventeenth century. Smith's Fort Plantation comprising 1200 acres was purchased by Warren from Thomas Rolfe, son of John Rolfe

A Domestic Scene at Jamestown About 1625

This representation of seventeenth-century home life was executed by the artist after a detailed study of artifacts and archeological remains found at Jamestown.

From a painting for Colonial National Historical Park by Sidney King.

Lee House (Chiskiac)—York County

The main building here shown was built about 1690 and was the home of the descendants of Henry Lee, who was in Virginia by the middle of the seventeenth century. The site, now within the United States Naval Mine Depot, was, before 1630 the territory of the Chiskiac (Kiskiacke) Indians. The wing attached is a modern addition.

tor of her deceased husband's estate, also pressed his suit and gained favor; whereupon, the cleric entered in the Court a suit for breach of promise. The contest over the widow finally was referred to the authorities in London, who declined to pass upon "so delicate a matter." Mr. Pooley, probably then finding his cause hopeless, withdrew his case in Court, and by 1625, the charming widow had married William Farrar.

Custom frowned upon the ladies of the seventeenth century going into Court. While the law required that they sign or give assent to their husbands' deeds for sale of land or property, when the time arrived that the deed must be acknowledged in Court, the wife requested some male friend to represent her and acknowledge the deed. Mrs. Elizabeth Sheppard, in 1654, wrote a note asking her "dear brother Cockerham" to represent her in Court. The same year, Daniel Llewellyn acknowledged a deed in Charles City Court, for his stepdaughters Sara Woodward and Anne Gundry.

Nothwithstanding the limitations put upon women of the seventeenth century, both by custom and by law, their husbands evidently had complete confidence in their discretion and their abilities to direct wisely the disposition of estates, which came into their hands. Their business experience was confined to household management and plantation activities, but these were enterprises of no mean proportions, and the successful handling of such matters by the women impelled the men, very frequently, to name in their wills their wives as executrices. At the same time, overseers were also named to assist in handling the details. Colonel Bridger named his wife Hester as executrix to dispose of his large landed estate and his extensive mercantile business, but directed that her brother and their mutual friend Arthur Smith assist her, which they did very ably.

Perhaps, there is no more outstanding example of an astute woman of the seventeenth century and her courage than that which the experiences of Sarah Bland set forth. She was the wife of John Bland of England, and the daughter-in-law of the well known merchant of the same name, who, as an active member of the Virginia Company of London, developed large plantation interests in Virginia, and a thriving mercantile business. Sarah Bland's only surviving son Giles had come to Virginia about the time of the untimely death of Theodorick Bland, who had managed the Bland interests in Virginia. Giles was a young "hot head," joined with the Bacon forces, and upon the collapse of that abortive revolution in the Colony, was apprehended, promptly condemned by Governor Berkeley's Court held at "Greenspring" and executed. Two years after her son's untimely death, and when some of the drastic measures confiscating the holdings of the deceased rebels had been lifted, Mrs. Sarah Bland, armed with power-of-attorney from her husband, crossed the seas alone to look into and settle the huge Bland estate. While she was in Virginia, her husband died in England, and Thomas Povey, who was named joint executor with her of her husband's estate, also conveyed to her power-of-attorney. She gathered the loose ends of the Bland holdings in Virginia and divided them among the heirs. An entry in the Isle of Wight County Court records, listing ten Bland plantations, indicates the proportions of her task.

Divorce in Virginia rarely occurred. There was no Ecclesiastical Court and, therefore, no source of authority to which dissatisfied couples might turn. The Governor and Council were vested with the power to grant separations, which were seldom sought. One of the very few cases of separation and remarriage was that of Elizabeth, sister of Colonel William Underwood and ex-wife of Doctor James Taylor. After petitioning the Governor and Council for a separation, she married as her second husband Francis Slaughter, merchant and planter of Rappahannock County, who was deceased by 1656, his will naming his wife and mother-in-law. Incidently, Elizabeth had, in all, four husbands before her death in 1673.

Lest conclusion be drawn that all women in Virginia were

ladies, women whose husbands had large plantations and who were to the manner born, acknowledgement must be made that there were some who were not gentlewomen. Some quarrelled outrageously with one another, some gossiped endlessly, and a few went to the extremes of dragging their husbands into Court to settle disputes with one another, thus, cluttering up the busy calendar of the County Justices.

The Court sitting at Westover in Charles City County, 3 August 1664, arrived at a means of disposing of these cases and silencing, perhaps, public display of temper. The ducking stool on Herring Creek had just been equipped, the year before, with new irons and so was in good repair. Whereupon, the Justices ordered that "Goody" Spencer and "Goody" Goodale for their "scurrilous brawls and frivilous litigations" be each ducked three times at the public place prepared for that purpose, at or near the next full tide, and that "each bear his own particular costs and charges."

The costs levied, the discomfort of being immersed, not to speak of the ridicule that such an event aroused on the part of the people assembled to witness the punishment, no doubt had a very sobering effect on tempers. There was also a ducking stool on Wormeley's Creek in York County, and another at Lynn-haven in Lower Norfolk. It would thus seem that these and similar cases were not altogether rare in the Colony.

SERVANTS

To interpret accurately the meaning of the frequently used term *servant* is a difficult matter. It appears to have covered a wide range of classifications in seventeenth-century Virginia. The designation was often used in the modern sense of employee and, occasionally, members of a family are listed in an enrollment as *servants* with the obvious meaning of dependents. This was the case in the muster of William Gany, 1625, whose child Anna heads the list of his "servants." Also, with Thomas Palmer and

47

his family, Richard English, aged eleven years, was living in 1625, but is listed as a "servant." Abraham Wood, aged ten years, is listed in 1625 as a "servant" of Captain Samuel Mathews. These children obviously do not come within the twentieth century meaning of the word.

Also, when individuals or groups of individuals sought to establish large settlements in Virginia, they sent over a company of men, and these men are listed as "servants," a term used in our modern sense of *employee*. The musters of Edward Bennett, Daniel Gookin and others present such lists. In the Bennett muster, Christopher Reynolds, evidently a head man in overseeing the creation of a plantation, comes under the designation. Also, Adam Thoroughgood, who later was named a member of the Council, is first mentioned in the colony under a list of "servants."

True it is that many young men bound themselves, by written agreement before departing from England to serve seven years in the colony, in return for passage and other considerations, granted at the conclusion of their terms. However, apprenticeship was the customary means, by which young men acquired knowledge, and some degree of skill from their elders. Young Robert Hallom, about 1640, was sent to England to live with relatives and receive some training. He, forthwith, was apprenticed to his cousin to learn the trade of a *salter*, and was described by the family as a "prettie wittie boy." When Doctor Pott came to Virginia, in 1620, he brought as apprentices to learn the art of apothecary, young Randall Holt and young Richard Townshend. Both youths became dissatisfied, and sought to break their agreements through petitions to the General Court, contending that Doctor Pott was not instructing them. However, the Court held the young men to their agreements. Later, Randall Holt married the heiress Mary Bayly, and became possessed of the large plantation, Hog Island on the James River. Townshend rose to prominence in the colony, also, having been named later a member of the Council. Often such young men were third or fourth sons in a family, and influence from overseas, as in Townshend's case, helped establish them in places of honor and authority in the colony.

Youths, who agreed by indenture to serve in Virginia, were the main source of help to the planters in the first half of the century. There was never a sufficient number to fill the needs in the Colony, and planters pleaded with the Company or with friends in England to send them "servants." In letters sent to authorities in England, 1622, the Rev. Richard Buck urgently requested that "servants" be sent to assist him in carrying on the work of his 750 acre plantation.

Letters from Kathryne Hunlock of England to her daughter and son by a prior marriage, Margaret and John Edwards, recorded in Northampton County, indicate the class of young people who often bound themselves to come to Virginia. Apparently, mother, son and daughter were educated, for the mother refers to the correspondence with them. In 1648, Kathryne Hunlock lists supplies she had sent to her daughter: eight yards of snuff colored silk mohair, an ell of taffeta, silver lace, four pairs of gloves, thread, hose, two taffeta hoods and two lace hoods with taffeta handkerchiefs, four pairs of shoes, one hundred needles, 5000 pins and "one green scarf for your husband." As the last entry shows, young Margaret did not long remain an apprentice, for she was redeemed from that status by a planter named Stephen Taylor, who, her mother wrote, she understood, was an "honest man and gave a great price" for her.

Later, Kathryne Hunlock wrote her daughter and her son regarding the daughter's inheritance from her deceased father. The son, incidentally, served out his time. The correspondence indicates that these were substantial folks, and the young people, probably having little to anticipate in an improved status in England, sought both adventure and a brighter future in Virginia.

Young orphans in the Colony, with no one to look to for

support, were bound out, this responsibility being accorded the vestry of the parish church. In 1646, the York records note that Ann Snoden, an orphan seven years of age, had no means left for her maintenance. Thereupon, she was bound out to Captain Nicolas Martiau for nine years, with the provision that he supply her with food, clothing, shelter, and give her a cow and a calf and maintain both during her apprenticeship, rendering an account annually to the court. In 1686, little William Hickman, a year old infant, was bound out to William Dods of Isle of Wight County to be in his care and service until he was twenty-one years of age.

Fewer than two score Negroes are listed in Virginia in 1625; they were not present in numbers in the Colony until about 1660. By then, they began to supplant white labor and were particularly useful in the tobacco fields, the latter an ever increasing source of revenue to the planter. Not all Negroes worked in the fields, however. In the inventory of Mrs. Elizabeth Digges' estate filed in York County, 1691, three sets of quarters for Negroes are listed: the home quarters where the house servants lived, the Indian field quarters where those working in tobacco lived, and the new ground quarters where were housed the Negroes doing the heavy work of clearing new ground, a constant operation in Virginia as the cultivation of tobacco quickly exhausted the soil.

As the Negroes took their places in the Colony as field-hands, house-servants and craftsmen, the white indentured servant vanished from the scene. As heretofore noted, the supply was never enough in the Colony to fill the demand. Moreover, young men, at the conclusion of their five or seven-year terms, received their allotment of clothing and supplies, usually a barrell of corn, agreed upon in the indenture, and joined the small-planter class in the Colony. Especially was this true when the indenture included a clause granting fifty acres upon completion of service.

Since Negroes were taught trades on the plantations and some of them became highly skilled in handiwork, the white artisan

50

had a difficult time in establishing himself in Virginia. There was practically no white artisan class. Small planters and their families acquired skills needed in their daily living, the Negroes becoming the craftsmen on the larger plantations.

THE HOUSEHOLD

The winters in Virginia, mild except for occasional freezes, with now and then snowfall during the three winter months, proved less arduous to the Englishmen than the two months of midsummer, when the mercury reaching into the nineties brought discomfort, especially since the men and women were clothed in the bunglesome garments, necessary in a cool zone frequently overhung with fog. The many open, pleasant months in the Colony made life out of doors a continuing pleasurable experience, when hunting, fishing, horse-racing and games could be indulged in freely.

Yet, living indoors in Virginia in the coldest weather was always cheerful. The land, heavily forested, yielded an ample supply of firewood of all sorts, and the necessity of clearing the ground, for the plantation homes and agricultural areas, kept heaps of wood at hand at all times. The earliest open fires of the primitive shelters as well as the great brick fireplaces later in the century, and the smaller hearths in every room of the affluent planters' homes, always diffused that glow of comfort instinctively sought, when the sun retreats. Before the burning logs of hickory and oak the families gathered. There could be no extravagance in the use of the abundant supply of wood, contrasting with the necessity to preserve fuel in England, as the forests there, even in the seventeenth century, were disappearing. Often, there were generous pots of walnuts and hickory nuts to crack on the hearth, as family and friends sipped from their pewter mugs the aging cider, pressed from apples gathered in nearby orchards.

In addition to the flaming hearth, the soft glow of the candle,

51

used for illumination in the seventeenth century, lent charm to the evening scene, as wanton shadows stood off in the room. Moreover, there was an elusive aroma from the candles, often made from the wax of berries, taken from the prolific growth of myrtle bushes about the Virginia waterways. This redolence, together with the clear light which the myrtle wax gave forth, made that candle popular in the evening; notwithstanding, both beef and deer suet were in use for candle making, and some candles were imported. All were held in candlesticks, made of wire, brass, pewter, copper, or iron, the more elegant, of silver, with snuffers of the same metals. In the very modest homes, the pine-knot served as a means of illumination, the turpentine in the wood fibers causing it to burn brightly until consumed.

Various house furnishings have been listed in the inventories or are listed hereafter. During the latter part of the century, particularly, it will be seen that these furnishings were as elaborate or as simple as in the comparable home in England.

Next to the fireplace, perhaps, the table adds more good feeling among family and friends than any other item of the household. To "gather around the board" was not merely a figurative expression in the early seventeenth century when the first tables were boards laid on trestles and set aside after meals. Table frames and planks were mentioned in a Lower Norfolk County inventory in 1643. Later, permanent legs were attached to the boards, and stretchers, fastened to them with pegs, kept the table steady. However, as the English began to fashion fine pieces of furniture, the table of various types found its way to Virginia and, by the middle and late seventeenth century, there were serving-tables, tea-tables as well as dining-tables. The four-times married Mrs. Amory Butler owned a rare item in an extension table.

Even the planter with a modest household owned table-linen. As heretofore noted, Joseph Ham possessed, before 1638, a dozen napkins and a table-cloth. The well-to-do planters, especially after 1650, brought with them, or sent for, a wide variety of table-linen, and both Mrs. Butler and Mrs. Digges owned napkin-presses, that of the former listed in 1673, and that of the latter in 1692.

Wooden trenchers and wooden spoons were the earliest table-ware in Virginia. Later, pewter-ware supplanted wood and while earthen-ware trays and pots were mentioned, in a few inventories, and were used in the dairy, and while earthen-ware was produced in the Colony by 1675, it did not come into general use for dining during the seventeenth century. Table-knives were not plentiful, nevertheless, various types of such knives are mentioned in inventories by the latter part of the century, black-handled, white-handled and ivory-hafted knives. The one rare item was the table-fork, which was not common even in England during the period. "Eating with the knife," a step beyond the use of the fingers, gradually became an established custom, and the practice has survived among the homely folks, despite the many varieties of forks available and in general use today.

The bed was a prominent item and the ticking of the best beds was filled with feathers, which assured a soft, comfortable, cosy resting place, especially in winter. There were no springs. The flock bed so often mentioned was less downy but comfortable, being filled with bits of wool, rags, milkweed or cattail-fluff, the latter in abundant growth near the fresh waterways. This was the "next best bed" which was a sufficiently important item to be left to heirs. Thomas Gibson, in 1652, bequeathed to his daughter his "best flock bed, with rug (used for covering), bolster, pillow and fine pair of Holland sheets." Sheets, variously mentioned, were of canvas or of Holland, generally, the latter, being an unbleached coarse linen. By the middle of the century, valances and curtains around the beds "to shut out the night air" were in general use. As soon as practicable, the English were bringing over their brass warming-pans with long handles. These perforated pans filled with warm embers were run in the beds just before the retiring hour. As the antecedent of the modern American electric blanket, they enticed the drowsy to bed. Retreating from the cheerful hearth, the would-be sleeper, then as now, had no fear of being aroused by the clammy chill of frigid bed-linen.

All colonists appear to have possessed chests of one kind or another, some plain, some carved. When the early planter obtained sufficient credit from his tobacco crop to indulge in a luxury, he acquired an innovation in a chest-of-drawers, where was kept the family clothing and the supply of materials on hand. Since dress was an important matter in the Colony, the looking-glass was indispensable. Occasionally, there was "a great looking-glass," but for the most part, the mirrors were small and stood on chests or chests-of-drawers.

Stools and benches were in use generally. Chairs, rare in England until the early part of the seventeenth century, nevertheless, found their way to Virginia about the time they came into use in England. However, chairs were scarce, and only the master of the house or his distinguished guest was accorded the privilege of being seated in them. The earliest chairs were cumbersome, being fashioned of oak with solid square backs, often panelled, and thus were known as "wainscot chairs." The seat was of wood and the bracing beneath made this article of furniture exceedingly substantial. Later in the century, a variety of chairs found their way to Virginia, caned chairs, leather chairs and Turkey-work chairs. The latter were those upholstered in hand-woven material imported into England from the Orient and then exported to Virginia. By the middle of the century, couches were listed and they were for the most part of the same construction as the chairs.

Lord De La Warr, who came to Virginia in 1610, sat in the Jamestown church in a green velvet chair. This is the first known mention of a chair in the Colony. In 1623, a wainscot-chair, owned by John Atkins of Jamestown, was bequeathed to his friend Christopher Davison, Secretary of the Colony.

In addition to the standard pieces of furniture aforementioned, luxury articles were imported during the latter part of the century. Mrs. Elizabeth Digges owned five Spanish tables, two green carpets and a Turkey-work carpet; Mrs. Elizabeth (Mason) Thelaball, of Lower Norfolk County, had among her possessions a small desk and a writing-slate. In the goods consigned, 1694, by Perry and Lane of London to Mrs. Elizabeth Woory, of Isle of Wight County, was a drugget.

The size of the homes varied from the simple one-room structures characteristic of the early part of the century to the Bridger home previously described, and Mrs. Digges' home of six rooms, hall, cellar, garret and detached kitchen.

In looking over the inventories of the seventeenth century planters, observation is inevitable that the kitchen area alone maintained its distinct character. Even among the well-to-do, beds were everywhere, irrespective of the number of rooms in use. Guns, swords, pistols, saddles, bridles, steelyards (scales) cluttered up the hall in the Bridger home.

Bathing facilities were meager. Copper and pewter basins were in general daily use, and also were employed for sponge baths occasionally taken in winter before the open fires. The chamber pots, frequently listed, served other necessary functions.

In the summer months, much of the cooking was done out-of-doors in huge pots slung from a tripod. The food for the servants went into a single pot, and their fare in "pap" was eaten in the open also, when the weather permitted. In the winter and during the cooler months, cooking was done on the hearth of an ample fireplace which customarily took up the greater part of the end of a room. If the family was of modest means, the kitchen area was the heart of the house. Here, in winter, was warmth, food and companionship. As the planter acquired numerous servants and preparation of food became an all-day matter, every day, the kitchen with its companion room, the buttery, was divorced from the house. Under this arrangement, the mistress of the household merely directed the preparation of food, the care of the dairy products, the salting of the meat, and the rendering of the lard.

Before the fire on the great hearth, meat on joints and fowl were trussed on spits, and to some small boy fell the task of keeping the spit turning. A drip-pan placed beneath caught the juices. Bakestones, griddles and clay ovens were at hand to stand on the hot embers, and later, ovens were built into the fireplaces. From cranes, simple at first and later with convenient arrangements for tipping, hung the pots for boiling. Bellows were at hand to enliven dying embers. On a rough table stood the brass mortar and iron pestle for mixing, the flesh-hook for handling meats, brass skimmer, rolling-pin, and other handy cooking utensils. Besides, in an adjoining space, there were pans, butter-pots, tubs and trays for the milk and milk products.

Water, which had to be drawn by hand from wells, except for an occasional windmill, was not a plentiful commodity. Therefore, the washing of clothes was not the semi-weekly operation carried on today with labor-saving devices. For the most part, it was carried on out-of-doors in clear weather, either at a nearby stream, or in the huge pots or tubs possessed by every family. Soap was brought into the Colony, and also was compounded from the animal fats available and the soap-ashes, which were plentiful. After soaking, the clothes were laid on boards and the grime driven out with "beetles" or paddles; then, the garments were hung up or laid out to dry or bleach in the sun. The few housewives, who owned napkin-presses, had the table-linen carefully folded, and placed, when damp, in the press in a pile. The board, screwed down firmly, eliminated the wrinkles, and the linen in some hours was smooth and ready for use. Also, various smoothing-irons and goffering (crimping)-irons, heated on the hearth were applied to garments. In all, however, laundering was a laborious process. Perfume, therefore, was a popular item in milady's toilet.

From time immemorial, the traveller, in sparsely settled areas in need of food and shelter at the end of the day, has always been made welcome, whether he was known or unknown. Moreover, there were no questions asked. Famed Virginia hospitality had its roots in this age-old custom, particularly as the early seventeenth-century traveller, often from overseas, could be sheltered nowhere else save at the homes of the planters. Although there were few inns, some taverns and ordinaries by the middle of the century, accommodations were poor and the well-to-do gentlemen preferred the warmth of the planters' hospitable homes to meager public accommodations. Nor was the entertainment of the unexpected guest a one-sided proposition, for visitors broke the daily routine of plantation life, bringing news from beyond and reports of what was happening in other parts of the Colony or overseas. Upon departure, the guest was sped on his way by his host or some member of the family, who accompanied him part way on his journey. In case he came by water, he was bade a final farewell from the planter's wharf.

Peter deVries, the Dutch sea-captain and trader, has left some early accounts of hospitality in Virginia. Although he recorded that the Englishmen in Virginia drove a close bargain in trade, and their acumen in that respect could not be surpassed, he was ever warm in praise of their hospitality. On his arrival in Virginia, 1633, he anchored off Newport News and visited there the Gookins. Later, when his ship sailed up the James River, he recorded that he stopped at "Littletown," the plantation of George Menefie, an early Virginia attorney, a prosperous planter and, said deVries, "a great merchant, who kept us to dinner and treated us very well."

When young Christopher Calthrope, aged sixteen years, came to Virginia in 1622, George Sandys, Treasurer of the Colony, proffered him the entertainment of his home and offered him his own room to lodge in. Although the young man declined, having other friends, Sandys saw to it that he was adequately cared for in the Colony.

The hospitality of Captain Samuel Mathews of "Denbigh" was widely known, even in England, where several, who had visited in Virginia, recorded the welcome they had received at his extensive plantation at the mouth of the Warwick River. In 1648, a writer, who signed himself Beauchamp Plantagenet, recounted his visit to Virginia where, upon arrival at Newport News, a few miles below "Denbigh," he was welcomed at the home of Captain Samuel Mathews and given "free quarter everywhere."

Virginia proved a haven to numerous Royalists as previously mentioned. Many who found it expedient to flee from England, about 1649, sought refuge in Virginia. Their coming was often kept secret, but they were accorded a warm welcome. Furthermore, when it was safe to make their presence generally known, they were received into official life in the Colony.

Among those who came and received welcome on the Eastern Shore at the home of Stephen Charlton were Colonel Henry Norwood, Major Richard Fox and Major Francis Moryson. Later they joined Colonel Mainwaring Hammond, Sir Henry Chicheley, Sir Thomas Lunsford and Colonel Philip Honeywood at Captain Ralph Wormeley's, on the Rappahannock River, and joined in the "feasting and carousing."

Governor Berkeley, a staunch Royalist, made the Cavaliers from across the seas particularly welcome, and as Colonel Norwood recorded, "house and purse were open to all such." Incidently, the term *Cavalier* loosely applied at times to all gentlemen who came to Virginia in the seventeenth century, irrespective of date, was a designation strictly applicable to those of a political party, loyal to the cause of Charles I, and it came into use during the Civil Wars in England nearly thirty-five years after Jamestown was settled.

58

Not only were guests from far-away places accorded the utmost in hospitality and given every indication that they were welcome, but visitors from neighboring plantations were often honored guests and they were ever the first consideration of their host. On 3 August 1658, Henry Perry of "Buckland" in Charles City County had been subpoenaed to appear in Court as a witness. On that day he had guests, so he addressed a polite note to the Court stating that he had a "company of friends" and therefore could not be present to testify as summoned to do. His courteous note was recorded in the County Court records.

The custom, occasionally adhered to, in the present time, of laying an extra place at the table for the possible coming of an unexpected guest from near or far, had its American origin in the seventeenth century in Virginia. More often then than now the extra place was filled at meal time.

FAMILY TRAVEL

Since all the early Virginia plantations, both large and small, were located either on the rivers or their estuaries, travel was almost entirely by sloop for distances, and by shallop or skiff for brief journeys. The families used such craft to attend church, and the planters to attend Court, the Council or sessions of the Assembly. In the latter half of the century, travel by horseback to the centers, or to attend funerals, or to visit friends, if not too far distant, became popular, especially as horses bred in the Colony had multiplied. The more affluent planters owned numerous horses mentioned in wills and, also, in inventories along with bridles, bits, stirrups and saddles.

In 1679, the Justices of Warwick County noted that a great number of small horses were running wild on "every man's land" and, in consequence, issued an order requiring that horses be penned, in order that the breed in the County "might not be crossed unfavorably." The same year, young Thomas Harris, son of Major William Harris of Henrico County, bequeathed to "my cousin Richard Ligon all my horses, mares or foals that can be proved to be mine . . . they not being given by my grandfather into the hands of the overseers." His grandfather, deceased about 1657, was, prior to that time, in possession of horses as the aforesaid entry shows. Colonel Joseph Bridger, of Isle of Wight County, owned fourteen horses at the time of his death. These are shown in the inventory of his estate entered, 1686. Thomas Cocke of Henrico County, who died in 1696, disposed of a large estate in his will, including his horses.

The absence of vehicles, except for a coach, a calash and carts, was due perhaps not so much to cost and the necessity for importing them as to the complete lack of passable roads in the Colony. Cartways, which were the worn and widened Indian trails, over which oxen hauled heavy loads, were the open ways over which travel by land could be undertaken. The bodies of the carts were made in the Colony usually and attached to wheels imported from England. Both the pillion and the side-saddle, the latter an item listed in the inventory of Mrs. Elizabeth Digges, 1692, were used by the women in accompanying the men on journeys. A pillion and a pillion cloth were bequeathed in 1652, by Captain John Upton, of Isle of Wight County, to his stepdaughter.

Notwithstanding the almost complete lack of highways, two Virginians are known to have owned vehicles for travel in the seventeenth century. The commission sent over from England to look into conditions which brought about Bacon's Rebellion complained, 1677, that Governor Berkeley had sent them from his plantation "Greenspring" to Jamestown, a distance of three miles, in his coach with the common hangman as a postillion. William Fitzhugh, a well-to-do planter of Stafford County, owned a calash, a sort of a cab imported from England.

Those who did not own horses considered it no hardship to walk miles to their destinations. Even so, the horse eventually became indispensable to Virginians of all classes, who became very skilled riders at an early age. Their adeptness in this as well as their knowledge in breeding, training and handling horses passed from generation to generation until the twentieth century. When the automobile supplanted the family surrey, and the network of hard surfaced highways succeeded to the shady, "woodsy," dirt roads, Virginia horses were retired from their long and noteworthy service to Colony and to State.

The Fashions

The earliest reference to a garment maker in Virginia is a petition entered in the General Court, 1626, through which Alice Boyse, widow, sought to reserve for herself and family indefinitely the services of young Joseph Royall, who had been brought to the colony by her late husband to make apparel for the family and such servants as Boyse retained under him.

The costumes of the seventeenth century followed precisely the prevailing styles in England though dress, through necessity, often was less elaborate. Travel, by the colonials back and forth to England, and the arrival of ships ladened with merchandise of all sorts, kept the planters and their wives abreast of the changing modes in dress. There were three major styles in the seventeenth century: the Jacobean, the Puritan and the elaborate dress of the Restoration.

These styles when reviewed today seem much too elaborate for a wilderness; however, news, circulated in England about the Colony, gave only encouraging accounts of an opulent land; thus, the men and women, who came, brought with them the essentials for a normal home life, and dress was an important aspect of ordinary living in England. Nevertheless, the authorities in Virginia took cognizance of the emphasis on dress, and, in order to encourage expenditures for necessities rather than the luxuries in clothing, the Assembly of 1619 enacted a provision taxing an unmarried man according to his apparel, and a married man according to the clothing possessed by himself and members of his family.

During the first quarter of the seventeenth century, men wore less elaborate costumes than the puffed, slashed modes of the Renaissance. The breeches were loose but covered the knee where they were fastened with buttons or a sash of ribbon, which often also decorated the instep of the high-heeled shoe. The doublet had fewer slashes and more padding. A stiff beaver hat, decorated with a white plume, rested on the head, with locks falling around the neck and often over the shoulders. The women as well as the men discarded the huge ruff, replacing it with a flaring collar known as the "falling band." The bodices of the women remained cylindrical in shape with sleeves tight from shoulder to elbow, falling loosely to the wrist where they were often finished with turned back cuffs. The farthingale gave way to the skirt, open from waist to hem in front, to show an elaborate petticoat. Both skirts were short enough to expose the instep and rosette or buckle on the shoe. The women forsook the caps formerly in vogue and adopted also the stiff beaver hats with feathers.

With the coming of Charles I to the throne, decorative features were added to the fashions. Colored ribbons, displayed in bunches at the knees, on doublets and as ties to hold back flowing locks, came into vogue along with flaring boots elaborately trimmed on the inner side of the flare, which was turned back. The women's costumes also underwent similar elaborations. Gloves appeared, also muffs, and the long circular cape was used as a wrap.

The severity of the regime, as established under the Commonwealth, 1649, was reflected in the dress of both men and women when all finery was discarded. Fabrics became somber in color and unpretentious in texture. Men had their locks shorn close to the head, and women returned to the simple caps or hoods, which held the hair close to the head. Virginia authorities took cognizance of England's turn towards simplicity in dress, and enacted a law prohibiting the introduction of clothing containing silk, or of silk goods in pieces, except for scarfs, silver and gold lace or ribbons interwoven with silver or gold. The law further provided for confiscation of silk articles brought into the colony against the law.

After ten years of this severity in dress, the populace in Virginia was ready for the change, which Charles II brought to England with his restoration as monarch. Having spent his exile in France at the brilliant court of Louis XIV, he brought with him, on his return to England, fashions which the colonials sought to adopt, although they were restricted somewhat because of the limited importations of silks and satins, elaborate colored ribbons, fine linen, beruffled shirts, and jeweled garters for the men.

The antecedent of the present-day coat worn by men was introduced in England by Charles II, having been patterned after a Persian coat brought to his attention. This coat, straight and collarless, was buttoned from neck to knees where it ended. The close sleeves were short, and finished with a deep turned back cuff, below which extended the lace ruffles of the shirt sleeve. In cold weather, a greatcoat of frieze (a shaggy-piled woolen fabric) was worn over the costume.

As the century wore on, women's dress became increasingly elaborate also. The skirts were looped high at the sides over trailing petticoats, the fronts of which were covered with fancy aprons of silk, linen or lace. The bodice was usually laced across the front with ribbons. Red-heeled shoes added a note of interest to milady's outfit.

Children's dress was patterned identically after that of their elders and, as may be imagined, very little freedom of movement was afforded.

The inventory of Philip Felgate, Gentleman, of Lower Norfolk County, entered on the records, 1646, shows that some of the more elegant styling in dress had been brought to the Colony at that time. He possessed a black cloth suit, two buff suits and a buff doublet, a short cloth coat and a coat of squirrel skins. To complete his costume there were two pairs of silk stockings, a pair of silk stirrup hose and black silk garters, five pairs of shoes, a beaver hat, a silver hatband. Evidently, Felgate was of the military service, for he had brought with him, to the colonies, a suit of black armor with a headpiece of white armor and a sword with a gold hilt. He owned also a musket and a rest for it, and was outfitted with a "suite of bandoleers," the latter, seldom listed in inventories, was a belt arrangement with loops, usually twelve, in which were fitted small pierced metal cases for carrying the slow matches (actually fuses), by which the charge for firing the gun was ignited. Three Monmouth caps, customarily worn by soldiers and sailors of the period, were among his possessions.

Major Croshaw's stepdaughter, upon the eve of departure from England, 1661, for Virginia, had been furnished with a scarf, a white sarcenet and a ducape hood, a white flannel petticoat, two green aprons, three pairs of gloves, along with a riding-scarf, a mask and a pair of shoes. Mrs. Sarah Willoughby of Lower Norfolk County, who died 1673, left a wardrobe valued at 14 pounds, 19 shillings. It included five petticoats, a red silk, a blue silk and a black silk, another of India silk and worsted prunella and a fifth of linen and calico. Also, the lady left a black silk gown, a scarlet waistcoat, a sky-colored satin bodice, a pair of red paragon bodices, a worsted mantle, two hoods, a striped-stuff jacket, seven handkerchiefs, six aprons, three of fine and three of coarse Holland.

Daniel Hopkinson, merchant, who died in Virginia, 1636, bequeathed to relatives and friends beaver hats, which had become very much the vogue during the reign of James I. Similarly, Robert Nickolson of London, who died on a voyage to Virginia, bequeathed to relatives in the Colony and to several of his associates, kid gloves, buckskin gloves and cordovan gloves.

In the seventeenth century clothes were not discarded as they are today for the garments, particularly for "Sunday wear" were carefully made. The more affluent planters had clothes made in England, William Fitzhugh having ordered from London, 1697, two suits, one for winter and one for summer.

It was not uncommon to find clothing bequeathed in wills. In 1676, James Crewes, ill-fated associate of Nathaniel Bacon in the Rebellion, bequeathed to young Daniel Llewellyn, his "best suit and coat."

The reader may wonder when and where jewels could be worn in seventeenth-century Virginia when, even at the close of the century, there were no centers, other than church at which a lady might attend to display her ornaments. Yet, the feminine frailty to covet the beautiful, whether in gems, in fine household furnishings, linens or silver, was perhaps even stronger than it is today. Possession of jewels was a mark of distinction, and, even though the precious baubles could be shown at functions but rarely, there was satisfaction in ownership and compensation in the admiration they elicited when worn.

The colonials possessed a great deal more jewelry than might be imagined. The opulence of the English merchants, trading in all parts of the world, in the late sixteenth and early seventeenth centuries, had enabled many to invest their surpluses in jewels, which fluctuated less than the unsteady values in the media of exchange, and, therefore, were an investment rarely decreasing in value. Moreover, jewels could be transported more readily than either gold or silver and, since the goldsmiths in England and Holland were the early bankers, they often advised their customers, particularly those about to embark upon a voyage to Virginia, to invest their profits in gems, easy to carry, not likely to fluctuate and always desirable.

The unusual purposes, to which jewels might be put, is recounted in a record of the sale of Mrs. Moseley's jewels to Colonel Francis Yeardley, who desired them as a gift to his wife, Sarah (Offley), widow successively of John Gookin and Adam Thoroughgood. William Moseley, his wife Susan and two sons Arthur and William arrived in Virginia, 1649, from Holland and settled in Lower Norfolk County. By reason of the family's "great

65

want of cattle," Mrs. Moseley, the following year, sold some of her jewels: a gold hat band enameled and set with diamonds, a jewel of gold (probably a pendant) enameled and set with diamonds, and a diamond ring. In a letter to the purchaser, she stated that they were genuine, having been examined by a goldsmith in The Hague, and were worth £11 4s. In exchange, the Moseleys received five cows and four oxen. Having still in her possession a ruby ring, a sapphire and an emerald ring, Mrs. Moseley could be gracious in parting with her gems and wrote Colonel Yeardley, she had rather his wife wear them than any gentlewoman she yet knew in the country, and wished her "health and prosperity" in her display of them.

At the same time, Mrs. Sarah Yeardley, the daughter of a well-to-do English merchant, and the spouse successively of three prosperous husbands, possessed other jewels. Her will dated, 1657, directed that her *"best* diamond necklace and jewell" should be sent to England to purchase six diamond rings and two black tombstones, the latter to be placed over her grave and that of her second husband, at the churchyard at Lynnhaven. Since all things ornamental were under a ban during the Commonwealth in England, it is not surprising that Mrs. Yeardley's necklace did not bring even the price of the two tombstones, which cost £19 7s., while the diamond ornament brought only £15. Yet, the tombstones, the inscriptions on which are extant, have left to posterity a permanent record of Mrs. Yeardley and her three husbands. After all, values are relative, and could Mrs. Sarah (Offley-Thoroughgood-Gookin) Yeardley view today the position she enjoys in the romance of Virginia's seventeenth century, she likely would not regret having traded diamonds for tombstones.

One of the earliest records of jewelry in Virginia is in the will of Mrs. Elizabeth Draper of London, dated 1625, in which she bequeathed to her granddaughters, Elizabeth and Mary Peirsey, daughters of the cape-merchant Abraham Peirsey, each, a diamond ring, Mary's set "after the Dutch fashion." Arthur

Smith I of Isle of Wight County made a bequest, 1645, of his "seal ring of gold," to his son Thomas. This much worn ring has passed from generation to generation, and remains today in possession of a descendent in the county in which the testator died. He also bequeathed mourning rings to the overseers of his will. Such bequests, as the latter, were frequently made and were inscribed, or carried a locket in which hair or some other memento could be placed. Mrs. Elizabeth Digges' inventory listed among her possessions: eight gold mourning rings, probably bequeathed to her by deceased relatives, a diamond ring, a small stone ring, a parcel of sea-pearls and a bodkin, the latter an ornamental hairpin.

In 1651, Robert Nickolson of London, merchant, dying on a voyage to Virginia, made en route a will with numerous bequests, among them, a diamond ring and a gold ring to Mistress Beheathland Bernard, daughter of Mrs. Mary Bernard and granddaughter of Robert Beheathland, who had come to Virginia with the first settlers in 1607.

In 1673, Mrs. Amory Butler, nee Elizabeth Underwood (Taylor-Slaughter-Catlett) left to legatees a collection of jewelry probably assembled, in part, during her four ventures in matrimony. These jewels included her wedding ring—to which husband is not known—two big stone rings, a blue enameled ring, two mourning rings, a small diamond ring and a large diamond ring, a small pearl necklace and a necklace with large pearls, a silver bodkin and a gilded bodkin, a pair of silver buttons, and a pair of silver buckles. The year following, Mrs. Rose Gerrard, widow, of Westmoreland County, made several gifts to her eldest daughter, Sarah, wife of William Fitzhugh, and among them were "one necklace of pearls."

Colonel Thomas Pitt, of Isle of Wight County, had the forethought, before he died in 1687, to leave to his wife her wedding ring along with her wearing apparel, and also title to her two diamond rings, an enameled ring, and a necklace of pearls. These items, otherwise, could have been accounted in his estate for division among heirs, for the law gave a woman no title to her possessions during the life of husband. Colonel Bridger also left to his wife, 1683, all "her apparel, rings and jewels."

Although clocks are listed in seventeenth century inventories, one of the earliest mentions of a watch was in 1697, when Richard Aubrey of Essex County, bequeathed two silver seals and his "pendilum watch."

FESTIVITIES, RECREATION AND SPORTS

That Christmas was an occasion to be enjoyed, both with comfort and merriment in the Colony, is indicated in an account, recorded in 1608, when a group of the first settlers in two ships undertook to visit Powhatan at his seat Werowocomoco on the Pamunkey (York) River. Setting sail from Jamestown they encountered rough weather and were forced to put in at Kecoughtan (now Hampton), where they spent Christmas with the Indians. Their scribes recorded that they were "never more merry, nor never had better fires in England than in the dry, warm, smoky houses of Kecoughtan."

Christmas in the seventeenth century was celebrated on the day known to the present as "Old Christmas," that is the sixth of January.

The dry, smoky houses of the Indians were long, arched structures with a framework of bent saplings, over which was secured a close covering of bark, while the roof was covered with mats or reeds. A fire built in the middle of the habitation, with smoke curling through an opening above, afforded both warmth and fuel for cooking. Mats and skins, hung at the entrance and exit, kept in the heat and also some of the smoke, but shut out the rough weather. Several families slept, ate and carried on their indoor activities in these ample shelters.

And, here, it was that the colonists, with only the Indian maids to provide feminine company, celebrated the first Christmas, of

68

which there is a record in the new world. After the feasting and the passing of the pipes, as a token of friendship, there was probably a customary Indian oration of welcome. Then, the Indian dancers appeared with their rattles, and beating time to the tom-toms with their feet, they gestured wildly with their arms. As a participant became weary, another took his place and this exhibition, first stimulating in its activity, then soothing in its cadence, carried far into the night, as, one by one, the audience of white men and natives drifted off to the hurdles that served as beds, and to sleep.

When the weather broke, and before the colonists resumed their journey, they likely were entertained by their hosts in a deer-hunt staged according to the Indian custom. Several Indian runners left, early in the morning, to drive up the deer and herd them on a narrow peninsula, of which there are many between the James and the York Rivers and elsewhere in Tidewater Virginia. Canoes, with native hunters and their white men guests, awaited in the waters nearby, and when the drivers, pursuing the deer, forced them into the water, the frightened animals were slaughtered in numbers. Ladened with the spoils, hosts and guests returned to the bark houses to cook and feast upon their game.

Firearms played an important part in all celebrations in the seventeenth century as every planter possessed one or more "pieces" which were used to give dash to the frolics. A proclamation, issued in 1627, warns against "spending powder at meetings, drinkings, marriages and entertainments." Thus, it is certain that the colonists were wont to assemble and celebrate as occasions warranted.

One of the most colorful of these occasions took place at Middle Plantation (later Williamsburg) in 1677; Sir Herbert Jeffreys, having been sent over with 1000 English soldiers to look into the state of affairs in Virginia and to put an end to the Rebellion led by Nathaniel Bacon, found Bacon dead and the Rebellion over. Shortly thereafter, Governor Sir William Berkeley, who had caused so much grief by hanging Bacon's chief associates, was summoned back to England, whereupon Jeffreys ordered a celebration. The King's birthday provided the occasion which he promoted, not only to honor the Sovereign but to assemble the people, to heal the wounds and promote peace with the Indians. Not only the colonists and the English troops gathered, but all the leading Indian chieftains and queens of Tidewater and their retinues were invited, and attended in ceremonial regalia. That there was not only formal recognition of the important day, but much firing of arms, drinking and hilarity on the side may be certain.

The planters of the Northern Neck, living in widely separated plantations, took steps in 1670, to bring together the families and promote sociability in the section. An agreement was entered into by Mr. Corbin, Mr. Gerrard, Mr. Lee and Mr. Allerton to build a banqueting house "for the continuance of a good neighborhood." Each man or his heirs in turn then would make "an honorable treatment fit to entertain the undertakers thereof, their wives, mistresses and friends, yearly and every year." This appears to be the antecedent of the modern country club.

In hunting, fishing, and fowling there was always ample out-of-door recreation at hand. In addition to the deer-hunts, there were often bear-hunts, and 'possum and 'coon-hunts were popular nighttime sports. On the latter occasions a party of men set out, preferably on a moonlight night, with their dogs. Having entered the woods, the dogs shortly took up the trail of their intended victim, while the men on foot followed the yelping dogs through the rough terrain. Finally the exhausted animal was "treed" and there the sport reached a climax. If the dogs were unable to reach their victim the tree was hastily felled, whereupon the pack of dogs made short work of the creature. In case the 'possum sought refuge in a hollow log, he was smoked out and the end was the same.

There was less excitement in hunting rabbits and squirrels,

70

and the pursuit of the fox had certainly not attained in the seventeenth century the social status that it enjoys in sections of Virginia today.

In fishing, many of the colonists acquired from the natives a skill in spearing fish, though netting them was far more general in the Colony.

Horse-racing as a regular sport was inaugurated in the latter half of the seventeenth century, although it does not appear that horses were bred and kept especially for racing in that period as they were during the eighteenth century. At the "race-paths" at "Malvern Hill," the Cocke plantation in Henrico, running the quarter of a mile was a popular contest.

Elsewhere, similar races were engaged in. In 1674, James Bullock, a tailor, was fined 100 pounds of tobacco in York County for racing his horse against Mr. Mathew Slader's horse, the decree reciting that it was "contrary to law for a laborer to make a race, being a sport only for gentlemen." Yet, Mr. Slader's intent to cheat at the race brought him a sentence of an "hour in the stocks."

On 10 May, 1676, Samuel Morris aged 27 years, deposed in Court about a horse-race run at Rappahannock Church.

Richard Ligon, to whom his cousin Thomas Harris bequeathed his "mares and foals" in 1679, was one of the racing enthusiasts of the Colony. He engaged in a horse-race and a controversy over it in 1678, and the following year he ran his horse against that of Alexander Womack, the wager being 300 pounds of tobacco. In 1683, Andrew Martin and Edward Hatcher put their horses in a contest in which the loser's horse was the stake to be won.

The colonists often were quarrelsome over their racing, and not infrequently, bets on horses were put in writing and recorded in the County records, that there might be no mistake in regard to the terms. These races elicited a great deal of interest on the part of the people in the countryside where they were staged.

For active recreation, bowling and tenpins; and card games of various sorts were engaged in, often at the ordinaries, and, since wagers on the games of which there are a record, were usual, they will be dealt with elsewhere.

MUSICAL INSTRUMENTS

Although existing records do not convey information, as to the part music played in the life of the Virginia planter of the seventeenth century, they do provide clues that music was enjoyed, and that a number of instruments were in the colony. Josias Modé, host at the French Ordinary in York County, whose widow, before 1679, married Charles Hansford, of York, owned two violins. It is reasonable to conclude, therefore, that guests at his hostelry were frequently entertained with music from that instrument. The virginal (a small rectangular spinet without legs) was the most common of instruments known to have been in possession of the colonists, while they also owned and played the fiddle, both small and large, the cornet, the recorder (a flageolet or old type of flute), the flute and the hautboy. These instruments in the hands of music lovers, frequently self-taught for the most part, entertained the planters' families and enlivened gatherings assembled for weddings and birthday celebrations. The hand lyre also was known in Virginia.

DRINKING HABITS

In their drinking habits the Englishmen in Virginia were no different from the Englishmen "at home." Accustomed to the use of "strong waters," they brought their tastes and their habits to the Colony. Hence, it is not surprising that the idea arose in England that the excessive sickness in Virginia was due to the substitution of water for beer in Virginia. This notion may have had substance at the time, since there were no sanitary precautions in the area of the shallow wells at Jamestown. Polluted water, no doubt, contributed to the prevalent sickness in the summer months, whereas the fermented and distilled waters disposed of impurities before they were ready for consumption and, thus, assured to imbibers a degree of safety from germ-bred diseases.

As early as 1609, the Virginia Company advertised for two brewers available to go to Virginia, and, in plans for the third and largest expedition sent under Sir Thomas Gates and Sir George Somers in 1609, provision was made to include experienced men, so that malt liquors could be brewed in the Colony and thus, the necessity of crowding the ships with such supplies generally in demand, could be avoided.

Prior to 1625, two brewhouses were being operated in Virginia, and twenty years later there were six. Also, the Virginia Assembly recommended that all immigrants should bring in their own supply of malt to be used in brewing, thus avoiding the use of drinking water, at least until they had become accustomed to the climate. At the same time, various products in the colony were found adaptable for producing drinks—persimmons for beer, sassafras for wine, and both barley and Indian corn were cultivated for brewing purposes.

Many of the planters developed their own facilities of one kind or another. Colonel Bridger had a malt-mill, and John Fisher a still. Cider was the established drink for family use and, as is known, gathered a good deal of strength as it aged. In addition, as trade between the Colony and the West Indies became brisk, quantities of rum (made from molassas) was brought in from that source. It became a common drink, was distributed especially for the use of servants, and was generally available in taverns, as was brandy distilled from peaches and apples.

The well-to-do planters were able to purchase the imported liquors and wines of a finer grade, sack and "aquavite" being the most popular in the early part of the century, while later, madeira, claret, and Rhenish wine became available. Some of the finest

73

wines were to be had at the taverns, including sherry, malaga, canary, and claret.

At meetings of public bodies, a supply of liquor was always provided for, ahead of time; Charles Hansford, of York County, agreed, in 1677, to supply the Justices meeting at the leased home of his deceased brother, a gallon of brandy at each session of the Court. One of the duties of the Auditor General of Virginia was to arrange for the supply of wines and liquors, which the august body of the Governor's Council of State expected to be on hand, while they were in session. While William Byrd I held that office, in the latter part of the seventeenth century, he ordered for their use, twenty dozen bottles of claret, six dozen of canary, sherry, and Rhenish wines, and a quarter of a cask of brandy.

Excessive use of liquors became the concern of the first Assembly sitting in 1619, who ordered that persons guilty of a first offense be privately reproved by the minister. In 1624, the church-wardens of every parish were ordered to report to the Commander of the plantations, in which the Parish lay, all persons who had imbibed too freely. By 1632, a fine of five shillings was set to discourage intoxication, and by the middle of the century, heavier fines were imposed.

The colonists were aware of the excessive use of liquor, particularly in gatherings. The will, of Edmund Watts of York County, dated 20 February 1675, forbade the serving of drinks at his funeral, the testator reciting that, inasmuch as he had observed "the debauched drinking used at burials, tending to the dishonor of God and religion, my will is that no strong drink be provided or spent at my burial."

In 1676, while Nathaniel Bacon held sway in the colony, efforts were made to suppress many long-standing abuses, among them, excessive drinking encouraged by the many taverns and ordinaries in existence. Laws were enacted, at that time, revoking the licenses of all inns, alehouses and drinking establishments,

74

except those at James City, and two at the ferries on the York River, where only beer and cider could be sold. This was the first recorded attempt at prohibition in Virginia. After the Rebellion was over, the enactment was modified, permitting the operation of two ordinaries in each county. Jamestown, the seat of government, was excepted from the limitation.

THE MINT JULEP

Just when the famous drink of the Virginia gentleman, the mint julep, was first mixed is not known, but the Colony possessed all the requisites during the seventeenth century. As heretofore mentioned, there was an ice house at Jamestown about the middle of the century. The fragrant mint grown in the planters' gardens, along with other herbs, has been known from time immemorial for its cooling refreshment, especially on a hot summer day. Brewed in a tea, mint was used both for a drink and, as a medicine, to induce mild perspiration and so bring down fever. The leaves, at times, made into a poultice, soothed inflamation.

Added to "strong waters" and ice, the mint with its delicate flavor, its cooling, soothing qualities, made the perfect drink for Virginia gentlemen during the humid midsummer. It was a favorite all-year-around, and three times a day. A julep before breakfast was usual, and grew into a custom, which lingered into the early twentieth century, in areas where the plantation manners persisted.

Although pewter was in general use for tableware during the period, glass was made in the colony, as early as 1609, and imported glasses not infrequently are mentioned in inventories. Mrs. Elizabeth Digges, of the "E D Plantation" in York County, left an estate in 1691 that included both earthenware and glasses.

With all the requisites at hand, it seems probable that the mint julep had its origin in the latter half of the century. If there was a company of friends, chilling the glasses ahead probably fell to a servant, who also was trained in the art of crushing the mint leaves with a bit of sugar, in each glass. Into this, at the proper moment was added the crushed ice to the brim and, as a jigger or two of liquor flowed over the ingredients, the glasses frosted and were topped with a sprig of mint. The pleasantness of the drink was not deemed its single virtue, for there was a very sincere belief in the efficacy of this refreshment in the promotion of good health and, particularly, in warding off the current fevers that plagued the lowlands.

GAMING

The inherent human trait of taking a chance for possible gain led the colonists to amuse themselves at games and sports, in which they invariably added a wager to lend zest to the occasion. This practice, generally prevalent in England, quite naturally was extended to the Colony, as the English established themselves with all their customs and habits in the new land. Betting was general at games and in sports, including horse-racing, heretofore dealt with, and cockfights.

Efforts to halt gambling apparently had little effect as most of it was carried on semi-privately. However, in 1646, Richard Smyth and John Bradshaw were fined 100 pounds of tobacco in Lower Norfolk County for "unlawful gaming at cards."

Unfortunately, knowledge of games played in the seventeenth century is available largely through the bets placed and subsequent accounts of these in the Court records. Doubtless many games were played among families on the plantations, as they are today, among friends, without wagers, but there was no occasion to record them. Thus, the fact predominates that cards, dice and ninepins were generally sources of amusement—for stakes.

Playing ninepins at the ordinary was part of the gentleman's day, when he came to the centers in the Colony, where these public places were established in numbers, after the middle of the century. At Varina, in Henrico County, Richard Cocke of

"Bremo" operated the ferry and also the ordinary there, where in 1681, his nephew young Thomas Cocke, Jr. is recorded as having been playing at ninepins for stakes with Richard Rathbone and Robert Sharpe. In 1685, in Henrico also, possibly at the ordinary, Giles Carter won 500 pounds of tobacco at dice from Charles Stewart. A card game called "putt" (put) and a game known as cross and pile (probably similar to "heads and tails") also were the media for bets, the bets no doubt affording the main interest in the game.

Luke Thornton and Peter Evans of Richmond County, "having agreed to play at cards at the game of 'putt'," had their arrangements with one another recorded, 7 February 1695, together with the consideration stipulated for the winner. The records do not reveal the outcome of the game nor any provision for enforcing by law the terms agreed upon. Nevertheless, the likelihood is that the winner collected, for, otherwise, the loser could be held up to public scorn.

FUNERAL CUSTOMS

When Abraham Peirsey, affluent cape-merchant, directed in his will, 1628, that he be buried "without any pomp or vainglory," he probably was protesting the tendency towards elaborate funerals, even in the early days of the Colony. It is not known whether or not his wishes in this respect were carried out; however, he was, no doubt, buried in his garden near his new frame house, as he requested.

On the other hand, Daniel Hopkinson, English merchant, who died on a voyage to Virginia, requested that he be "decently" buried at the Kecoughtan (Hampton) church, in accordance with the customs prevailing in the area. The amount spent on his funeral is an item in the accounts of the *Tristram and Jane*, on which he had crossed the seas as supercargo.

Arthur Smith of Isle of Wight County, in his will dated 1645, directed that he be "buried by my late beloved wife," and Richard

Cocke, of "Bremo" on the lower James River, requested in his will, dated 1665, that he be "interred in the orchard near my first wife." Doubtless, the second wife, mother of several of his younger children, carried out her husband's wishes and permitted her deceased mate whatever comfort there might be in the fore-thought of resting in the cold, dark ground beside the lovely lady he had first chosen to be his bride.

At every plantation there was a family burying ground, not far distant from the house, and usually in or near the garden, where the blossoms carefully nurtured, brightened the last resting places of deceased members of the family. The plantation bury-ing-ground originated through necessity rather than in senti-ment. In the seventeenth century a real problem would have been posed by any attempt to transport the deceased and the funeral procession to the distant churchyard.

The Swann family, living across from Jamestown at "Swann's Point," buried deceased members on the plantation and, for al-most three centuries, their graves could be identified. The Travis family living on Jamestown Island and near the church there, nevertheless, interred their dead in the family burying-ground at the lower end of the island, and some of the later marked graves may still be identified.

Markers in the Jamestown church, some over unknown graves, indicate the practice of burying persons, probably those of im-portance, within the church, as was often done in England. The Knight's tomb in the Jamestown churchyard is believed to be that of Sir George Yeardley, appointed Governor of Virginia, 1618, and deceased, 1627. Colonel John Page, who gave the land on which Bruton Parish Church in Williamsburg is built, was buried in its churchyard, as were his wife and son Francis. The stone, placed in memory of Colonel Page, was later removed and placed within the Church.

While funerals in seventeenth-century Virginia were solemn occasions, there was an inescapable social aspect to the gatherings of family and friends, who assembled from the countryside, both to comfort the bereaved and attend the departed on his last journey. When a planter or a member of his family died, messengers were sent out at once by sloop or shallop up and down the rivers or later, overland, on horseback. If the family bore arms, the hatchment, emblazoned with this emblem, was hung upon the door. Incidentally, the only known hatchment, that has survived in Virginia, is in possession of the Carter family at "Shirley" in Charles City County.

At once, preparations were begun to accommodate the relatives and friends who were sure to assemble for the last rites. Coming from a distance, they would be hungry upon arrival, and not only was a great amount of food prepared but the cellar was explored for its contents of drink, which the company expected to be brought forth. Occasionally, a man, in making his will, directed what should be spent for the "funeral meats" and drink, although Edmund Watts of York County, in 1675, forbade the serving of drinks at his funeral.

At the final rites for John Smalcomb in 1645, the company consumed a steer and a barrel of strong beer, the cost of which amounted to 960 pounds of tobacco, while the coffin cost only 250 pounds. The gathering assembled in 1678, for the funeral of Mrs. Elizabeth (Worsham) Epes, widow successively of William Worsham and Francis Epes of Henrico County, consumed a steer, three sheep, five gallons of wine, two gallons of brandy, ten pounds of butter and eight pounds of sugar.

The firing of guns was accepted as a regular feature of a funeral, and at the Smalcomb rites the powder spent amounted to twenty-four pounds of tobacco. In order to curb the waste of ammunition at entertainments, the Assembly, in 1655, passed an act forbidding its use on occasions except at "marriages and funerals."

In addition to expenditures as aforesaid and for the coffin, the latter usually made by some local carpenter, there were costs for notifying the countryside, costs for mourning bands, sitting up with the corpse, and the fee for the funeral sermon. If burial was in the churchyard, there was the cost of digging and filling the grave. The cost of a winding sheet of Holland (coarse unbleached linen), in 1652, was 100 pounds of tobacco. The cost of the funeral sermon in two instances in York County in 1667, was two pounds sterling each and in 1690, five pounds sterling.

As there were no undertakers, the laying out of the corpse was a tender ministration for which some close friend of the family volunteered. The technique for this service was passed from generation to generation and only in comparatively recent years has that custom been abandoned altogether.

The company of relatives and friends, who gathered for the funeral occasion, remained for several days and were, of course, fed and housed at the expense of the deceased's estate.

The law required that servants be buried in public cemeteries established for the purpose. This decree issued in the seventeenth century followed several scandals, occasioned by private funerals of deceased servants. In order to remove all possibility of suspicion, prior to burial, several neighbors were summoned to view the corpse, if death occurred under extraordinary circumstances, and to accompany the body to the grave. That such precautions were taken as early as 1629, so that possible murder would not go undetected, is shown in testimony before the General Court at Jamestown after the newly-born bastard child of a servant girl was found dead. Several persons were called as witnesses, and when evidence was produced that the child might have been born alive, the serving maid's master was required to give bond for her appearance at a higher court.

TOMBSTONES

The well-to-do planters or their families invariably saw that appropriate tombstones with proper inscriptions—lengthy ones, characteristic of the day—were duly placed. Some of these stones remain with barely legible inscriptions; others, the inscriptions on which, fortunately, were copied in a past era, have disappeared altogether. The oldest tombstone in Virginia with a legible inscription is that of Mrs. Alice Jordan at "Four Mile Tree" in Surry County. The inscription, reciting that she was the wife of George Jordan, gives praise in verse to her virtues.

Tombstones in the seventeenth century were real memorials, often giving parentage of the deceased, the name of wife or husband and the number of children. Furthermore, there was, as aforesaid, a eulogy of the deceased and, for men, an account of public service rendered.

With a great deal of pride in family background, those Englishmen in Virginia, whose families were entitled to bear arms, invariably had these cut upon the stones along with the lengthy inscriptions. The stones were ordered from England. As previously mentioned, Mrs. Sarah Yeardley, in 1657, directed that her executor sell her jewels and purchase in England stones for herself and her second husband. Her son, by the first husband, Adam Thoroughgood II of Lower Norfolk County, was equally zealous that proper memorials be placed and directed his executrix (wife), in his will, dated 1679, to have his body interred in the Church at Lynnhaven, and "cause a tombstone of marble to be sent for, with coat of arms of Sir George Yeardley [his wife's father] and myself." Unfortunately, these tombs together with the site of the old Lynnhaven Church, have been washed beneath the waters of Lynnhaven Bay.

The tombstones bearing coats of arms of George Read deceased, 1671 and his wife Elizabeth, daughter of Nicolas Martiau, uncovered during excavations at Yorktown in 1931 were removed to the graveyard surrounding Christ Church. The inscriptions, badly worn, were recut with information then in hand; however, the dates since have been found to be slightly in error. The tombstone of William Cole II, Secretary of State for the Colony, 1690, erected after his death, 1694, at "Bolthorpe," bore the

81

Cole coat of arms, accompanied by a lengthy inscription, reciting in part that the deceased was "unspotted on the bench, untainted at the bar." Unfortunately, when the graveyard lay neglected for many years and overgrown with vines, other ancient stones, placed there, were broken and portions of them, from time to time, carried away by fishermen to be used as mooring stones for their boats.

Theodorick Bland, deceased, 1671, was buried in the old churchyard now adjacent to the garden at "Westover." The inscription in Latin on his tombstone recites that it was erected "by his most disconsolate widow, a daughter of Richard Bennett Esq." Lewis Burwell, deceased 1653, was buried at his plantation, "Fairfield," in Gloucester County, and the tombstone erected to his memory, bearing arms, recited that he was descended from the ancient family of Burwell of Bedford and Northampton, England.

The tomb of Alice (Lukin) Page, wife of Colonel John Page, stands facing the west entrance to Bruton Parish Church in Williamsburg and is unique in that it bears the Lukin arms alone, indicating that the deceased was the sole heir of her father and thus entitled to his arms. Otherwise, the arms cut upon her stone would have been quartered with those of her husband.

The inscription on the tombstone of Edward Digges, buried on the "E D Plantation" (later, "Bellefield"), 1676, recited that he was the father of six sons and seven daughters. The broken tomb of Major Miles Cary I in a secluded spot in the area of his former plantation, "Windmill Point," in Warwick, was restored some years ago. The inscription relates, in part, that he was killed by the Dutch, during a foray which they made into Hampton Roads in 1667.

BIBLIOGRAPHY

Bruce, Philip A. *Economic History of Virginia in the Seventeenth Century*. New York, Macmillan, 1895. 2 vols.

Hening, W. W. *Statutes at Large of Virginia, 1619-1792*. 13 vols.

Jester, Annie Lash, and Martha Woodroof Hiden. *Adventurers of Purse and Person, Virginia, 1607-1625*. Printed by Princeton University Press. 1956.

Smith, John. *Travels and Works*. Edited by Edward Arber. Introduction by A. G. Bradley. Edinburgh, 1910. 2 vols.

Stanard, Mary N. *The Story of Virginia's First Century*. Philadelphia. 1928.

Strachey, William. *The Historie of Travell into Virginia Britannia*. Edited by Louis B. Wright and Virginia Freund. London. 1953.

Virginia, Colony. Council and General Court Minutes, 1622-32, 1670-1676. Edited by H. R. McIlwaine. Richmond. 1924.

Virginia Company of London. Records. Edited by Susan Myra Kingsbury. Washington. 1906-1935. 4 vols.

Virginia County Court Records. Manuscript volumes in Archives Division, Virginia State Library, *passim*.

83

INDEX

85

Old Christmas, 68
Old Point, 5
Orchards, 22, 23
Orient, importations from, 40
Pace, Izabella, 9; Richard, 9
Page, Alice (Lukin), 82; Frances, 13; Francis, 78; Colonel John, 78
Palisades, 16
Palmer, Thomas, 47
Pamunkey (York) River, 68
Particular Plantations, 11, 12; Supplies for, 12, 13
Patience, 4, 6
Pease Hill Creek Mill, 28
Peirce, Joane, 6; Mrs. Joane, 6, 22; Captain William, 6, 22
Peirsey, Abraham, 14, 20, 23, 66, 77; Elizabeth, 66; Mary, 66
Peirsey's Hundred, 16
Perry, Henry, 59; Micajah, 36, 37; William, 9
Perry and Lane, 55
Peru, 1
Pettigrew, Andrew, 30
"Pickthorn Farm," 29
Pitt, Colonel Thomas, 37, 67
Plantagenet, Beauchamp, 58
Plantation Life: Calthrope, 31-34; Bridger, 34-41
Planters, independence of, 27-30
Pleasants, John, 37
Pocahontas, 22
Pollentine, Mrs. Rachel, 21
Pooley, Rev. Greville, 44, 45
Population 1625, 15
Poquoson, 28; *see also* New Poquoson
Poquoson River, 31; New, 19; Old, 19
Pott, Doctor John, 20, 48
Pottery kiln, 29
Povey, Thomas, 46
Powell, Colonel, 40; Captain Nathaniel, 13
Powhatan, 68
Purefoy, Lieutenant Thomas, 31
Ragg, Thomas, 32

Rappahannock: Church, 71; County, 46; River, 58
Rathbone, Richard, 77
Raymer, Adam, 14
Read, Elizabeth (Martiau), 81; George, 81
Recreation, 68-72
Reynolds, Christopher, 48
Richmond County, 77
Roanoke Island, 1
Robins, Mary, 43
Rolfe, John, 22; Thomas, 22
Rolfe House, 21
Rookings, William, 24
Rowles, Jane, 14; Richard, 14
Royalists, 2, 34, 58
Royall, Joseph, 61
St. Luke's Church, 34
Salford, Joane, 8; Robert, 8; Sarah, 8
Sandys, Sir Edwin, 10; George, 16, 17, 57
Savage, John, 43
Scales, 18, 55
Seaventure, 4, 6, 30
Servants, 18, 19, 47-51, 80
Sharpe, Robert, 77
Sheild, Robert, 43
Sheppard, Mrs. Elizabeth, 43, 45
"Shirley," 79
Silk culture, 17
Skimeno, 28
Slader, Mr. Mathew, 71
Slaughter, Elizabeth, 46; Francis, 46
Smalcomb, John, 79
Smith, Arthur, 45; Arthur I, 67, 77; Major John, 34; John of Nibley, 12; Captain Roger, 16; Thomas, 67
Smith's Fort Plantation, 21
Smith's (Southampton) Hundred, 11
Smyth, Richard, 76
Snoden, Ann, 50
Somers, Sir George, 6, 73
Southampton Hundred, 11
Southey, Thomas, 11

89

Woodward, Sara, 45
Woory, Mrs. Elizabeth, 55
Wormeley, Colonel Christopher, 37; Captain Ralph, 58
Wormeley's Creek, 47
Worsham, William, 79
Yeardley, Colonel Francis, 65, 66; Governor Sir George, 4, 10, 11, 21, 22, 78, 81; Mrs. Sarah, 66, 81, *see also* Offley
York: County, 28, 30, 32, 33, 42, 44, 47, 50, 71, 72, 74, 75, 79, 80; River, 31, 69, *see also* Pamunkey River
Yorktown, 81
Young, Richard, 23

www.ingramcontent.com/pod-product-compliance
Lightning Source LLC
Chambersburg PA
CBHW060806110426
42739CB00032BA/3122